Heavenly Father certainly blessed
me when I married your son
and you became my mother.
Merry Christmas mother
your daughter
Bonnie

Remarkable Stories from the Lives of Latter-day Saint Women

Remarkable Stories from the Lives of Latter-day Saint Women

Compiled by Leon R. Hartshorn

Published by Deseret Book Company, Salt Lake City, Utah 1973

Library of Congress Catalog Card No. 73-87239
ISBN No. 0-87747-504-0

Second Printing 1973

Printed in U.S.A.

Contents

Mary Bailey Smith

Mary Fielding Smith

Sarah Farr Smith

Eliza R. Snow

Belle S. Spafford

Biographical Sketch

ELAINE CANNON

Elaine Anderson Cannon is recognized as one of the nation's leading personalities on the problems of teenagers and women's affairs.

A native of Salt Lake City, she attended the University of Utah, where she served as president of the Associated Women Students, was elected to such honor societies as Beehive and Mortar Board, and served as president of Chi Omega. She received her bachelor of science degree in sociology.

Listed in *Who's Who in American Women*, Mrs. Cannon has been a delegate to the White House Conference on Youth. She has been honored for "fine editorial support of worthwhile youth activities," and was presented a special citation by *Seventeen*.

In recent years she was named Exemplary Woman of the Year at Ricks College and was also so honored at Idaho State University and Weber State College. She has won first place in the National Press Women's contest in writing for youth and has received the all-Church honorary Golden Gleaner award.

Elaine Cannon appeared on television and radio and for many years was youth editor and daily columnist for the *Deseret*

1

News, where she also served as society and women's editor. She has written several books and numerous articles for professional and national publications. Her church service has included the MIA general board, the Church Youth Correlation Committee, LDS Student Association, and international adviser to Lambda Delta Sigma. She is an instructor in continuing education for both Brigham Young University and University of Utah.

Elaine Cannon and her husband, D. James Cannon, have six children.

ELAINE CANNON

"Bigger Inside"

$\mathbf{A}$s recently as this morning in our family prayer, our fourteen-year-old son asked Heavenly Father to bless me in this assignment and then gave me a very hard-to-come-by little peck on the cheek (for which I was very grateful and didn't make too much of a fuss over or I would never get one again!). I later thought, thinking of the priesthood, what a sweet thing this was for me to have a son holding the priesthood to ask the Lord to bless me.

In our home we had a boy and then four girls and then this younger son. It has always been our custom, when the daddy wasn't home, that the next member of the priesthood took over in leadership—asked someone to ask for a blessing on the food, helped us with the decisions, helped mother sit down, or whatever. It is a part of the training for the girls, as well as the boy, to give proper status to the priesthood in the house. You see, I sensed this morning how our young son felt bigger inside because of this thing he was able to do on this important day in our lives, to ask the Lord to bless mother as she served Him here today.

"Male, Female, and the Lord," *Speeches of the Year*, Brigham Young University, February 10, 1970, p. 4.

3

"This Is What Good Men Do"

I have a confession to make here today. It is how I learned a valuable lesson about wives and priesthood service and how thankful I am that I learned it early in our marriage. We had been married five years, had four children, had a little house that was empty of furniture, with lots of debts and big dreams, and my husband was called to be a bishop. . . . I remember the first thing that I said to him, "Do they call people to be bishops who don't have any carpeting or money?" And he said, "Yes, here we are, a shining example."

Well, I don't know how you girls dream about what it will be like when you are married, but when I was young I dreamed that Sunday would be a beautiful day. The children would be dressed in their best clothes and we would come home from church and sit down at a table beautifully set, a delicious dinner that had been well managed by mother, you know, and have scintillating conversation at the table. It isn't like that!

This particular Sunday everything was set up and my husband didn't come and he didn't come and he didn't come. The colder the dinner got and the crosser the children were, the more annoyed I became. Finally, I fed the babies and put them down for afternoon naps. Then I waited and waited and I was really upset! And then I began to feel hungry. It was that late. Suddenly I thought, "If I'm hungry, this giant of a man I'm married to (six-foot-six) ought to be famished by now. If he could possibly make it home, he would be home to eat, if for no other reason." And this is when my mood started to change and I realized that he *would* be home if he could, so he couldn't be home. It must be something important. By the time he came home my attitude had changed and I was ready to greet him properly. I brought him in, fussed over him, fed him, and I listened to him, and so on. When this was over he turned to me very soberly and said,

"Elaine, today I had one of the most spiritual experiences of my life."

(What had happened was one of his counselors was suffering with ulcers and was having severe hemorrhages. These brethren had given him a blessing and he had been healed on the spot.) "What if I had come home and *you*, my wife, had spoiled my mood!" explained my husband. Oh, what if I had! You know, my eyes filled up with tears and I smiled as if I were an angel on earth, but, oh! inside I was so thankful to my Heavenly Father that I got hungry and then smart. What a dreadful thing if a man couldn't come back to his particular corner of heaven on earth and be accepted and supported in what it was he was trying to do.

Girls, when you are kneeling in prayer as I am sure you are doing night and morning in this institution, asking that you'll get a good man, I hope you'll remember my story. I don't want to hear any complaints the rest of your life because your man is doing some service for the Lord. This is what good men do! So pray for him. Live worthy of him, and then grow up in the gospel so that you can support him.

"Male, Female, and the Lord," *Speeches of the Year*, February 10, 1970, pp. 5-6.

ELAINE   CANNON

"Just Pray That I May Be Able to Sleep Through the Night"

Last month in our fast meeting a young woman stood up under great difficulty, the first time she had been able to since her husband passed away some time before. She told of his teaching her a powerful lesson just before he died. They hadn't been married very long when he became critically ill. In the last stages of his illness he was suffering beyond belief, and this young wife was really desperate.

This particular night she knelt by the side of his bed and cried out loud to the Lord as only a loving woman can do who is full of anxiety, full of demands, begging, almost scolding the Lord to hear her and answer her prayers to help her husband . . . to heal him. She was near hysteria with her pleadings. It was then she felt a touch on her shoulder. It was her husband trying to calm her. She looked into his eyes and he said to her, "Please, dear—just pray that I may be able to sleep through the night."

As she bore her testimony she continued, "That sweet sustaining lesson taught me that you don't ask for the whole world; you don't demand for your own will to be done, but you just pray for strength that you can meet the tests of the day. And that lesson from my husband just before he died has helped me to sleep through the night."

"Male, Female, and the Lord," *Speeches of the Year*, February 10, 1970, p. 4.

MARGERY CANNON*

"We Cannot Ignore Our Little Ones"

A young mother leaving for a week-end trip deposited her eighteen-month-old baby in the arms of his grandmother.

"Thanks, Mom, you're a dear. . . . Oh, one more thing. Before you feed him, would you please put his little hands together and help him say a simple blessing on his food. We have family prayer with him at night, too. If you and Dad wouldn't mind kneeling by the side of his crib for prayers—he's used to it. I think it would help him feel more secure."

As her daughter disappeared down the driveway, the grand-mother thought about the request. What wise parents they are, she decided. A habit in the making at eighteen months will be a way of life at eighteen years. She couldn't help but contrast her daughter's philosophy with that of the young mother next door.

*Margery Sorensen Cannon, a daughter of Mr. and Mrs. Horace A. Sorensen, is the wife of William W. Cannon. They are parents of eight children—six boys and two girls—and have one grandchild. Brother and Sister Cannon served a mission together to Hawaii shortly after their marriage. A writer who has had many articles published in Church and national magazines, she has been a member of the Primary general board and of the *Children's Friend* editorial board and is now a member of the Church's Adult Correlation Committee.

7

"I'm going to work until my baby is two and a half. Before that time babies don't really understand who you are or what life is all about, anyway."

President J. Reuben Clark, Jr., once stated: ". . . the Lord has made clear in his revelations that, from earliest infancy, children must be taught in the principles of the gospel and in the doctrines of the Church, else 'the sin be upon the heads of the parents.' "

We cannot ignore our little ones. They are eager and willing to learn. And if we teach the gospel truths early enough, surely, when our toddlers have grown tall, they will not depart from them; surely they will not only be resurrected, but exalted and have "glory added upon their heads for ever and ever." And we, as parents, will be blessed with the realization that we fulfilled our pressing obligation to the Lord.

Relief Society Magazine, May 1970, p. 340.

HARRIET CARTER *

"She Hastily Grabbed the Heavy Door"

One night Harriet Carter, who happened to be alone at the ranch except for her small children, was awakened by a terrible commotion out in the nearby corral. Cows were bellowing, calves bawling, and a most awful din broke the stillness of the night in the lonely ranch home. Accepting her responsibility as head of the house in the absence of any men folk, she struck a light, hastily dressed herself, and proceeded to investigate the cause of the trouble and disturbance.

As she hastily grabbed the heavy door, after warning the children to lie quiet until she returned, she found it held fast. Surprised but undismayed, she grabbed for the handle again, only to find that it would not budge an inch to her healthy grasp. Sensing that something was wrong, she quickly surveyed its surroundings to see if any heavy object could be holding it so tightly, but could find nothing whatever that should have prevented it from opening it as usual. A few more strenuous jerks, however, soon convinced her that she was locked tightly in the

*Harriet Carter, who was born on July 13, 1835, was married to William Carter. They had seven children.

cabin, with no other openings large enough for her to get through. Stirred on by the uproar outside, she tried to peek through the tiny cracks, but only the blackness of the night met her anxious eye. After repeated attempts to open the fastened door, she finally gave up and went back to bed, after the bellowing and bawling had died down to an occasional snort of fear from one of the animals.

Awakening early, she at once dressed and upon going to the door, found that it yielded readily to her touch and swung silently inward on its hinges. Looking quickly around, she proceeded to the corral. There, to her surprise and horror, she found the fresh remains of a newly slain calf, surrounded by numerous cougar tracks. So the lion had come to her own yard for the kill. Returning thoughtfully to the house, she carefully studied her door and wondered if a kind and merciful Providence had caused her door to be held fast.

Kate B. Carter, *Heart Throbs of the West* (Salt Lake City: Daughters of Utah Pioneers), vol. 3, p. 336.

SHIRLEY CASPER *

"I Enjoy Being a Mormon"

I've said on many occasions that I was ready to join The Church of Jesus Christ of Latter-day Saints several years before Bill was. I had had much more introduction to the Mormons than Bill had had. When I was a young girl, some of my mother's dear friends were Mormons. When I grew up and later when we were married, I had many friends from around the country who were Mormons.

When Bill won the U.S. Open in 1959 and we were able to spend a little more time in Salt Lake City, Utah, I was well enough versed in religion to be able to make some rather interesting observations. It was about that time that I looked quite intently at Mormonism. I wanted to know about it, and the more I learned, the more I wanted to continue to learn.

There was a frankness about Mormons—not in a brash sort of way, but rather in the manner in which each member seemed

* Shirley Ann Franklin Casper was married to golfer William (Billy) Earl Casper, Jr., on June 28, 1952, in San Diego, California. They were baptized into the Church in January 1967; at that time they had three children of their own. They have since adopted five more children. Sister Casper was selected as the California and then the National Young Mother of the Year in 1970-71. Active in community affairs, she also teaches social relations in the Chula Vista (California) Ward Relief Society.

confident that what he was doing about religion was what he wanted to do.

They seemed to live better than other people, to be prosperous—and I don't mean from a money standpoint. They were healthy, happy, busy people. They were involved with their families. If you met a Mormon, you usually met his family.

I liked the Church's youth programs. I favored the Tabernacle Choir and always wanted to sing in it. No one forced his religion on us. We just seemed to enjoy our Mormon friends as they were.

I remember some of the first parties in Utah. There seemed to be less drinking and certainly less smoking. After you sit in smoke-filled rooms night after night, day after day, you enjoy the luxury of clean air.

To repeat, I liked the way the Mormon people were living. This aroused my curiosity more than ever.

The fact that Bill was slower to come to the point of conversion than I was is very understandable. As I have searched the scriptures and become more learned in the gospel, I find that this had to be.

I would have liked to have gone with Bill into the temple long before we got there, but he was not prepared for it. Our Lord and Savior is kind to us in that way—he gives us no more of his laws than we have the capacity to observe. We all had to progress to that capacity before we could be given what we have now.

When Bill said he would be baptized, I knew for sure he meant it. No one knows Billy Casper as I do. I've always liked him just the way he is. When Billy makes up his mind he wants something, he usually gets it. He hadn't made up his mind on church matters when I first did, so I waited.

Linda, Billy, and Bobby waited too. I believe Linda could sense my anxiety. And maybe big Bill could. But that wait, only for a few more months, was worth it. Just as Bill steps up to the golf ball and hits it, so he had made up his mind as he approached his new challenge, and when he took the promise, he meant it.

New worlds have opened to us. I was able to tract with some of the lady missionaries in Hong Kong—just to learn about the missionary program.

With our golf we have gone to far places of the world, and we find the Saints the same loving and kind people wherever they go. They are not just golf fans, people in Bill's gallery. They are our brothers and sisters in the gospel—the same brothers and sisters we had in the spirit world as sons and daughters of our Father in heaven.

I have found that the Church is not just a society. It is a learning process. From here we take all we have known, good and evil alike, and go to the next place. We will be at that time no more than we have been here, except as we are received in the glory of God, if that is what we have earned.

It is satisfying to me to believe that we shall know the people again we have known in so many places in the world. Before I became a Mormon I couldn't fully appreciate the depth of the gospel plan. Now it seems so real, so reasonable. And whenever I read the scriptures now, they offer me more light than they ever did before.

We Caspers have found out that if we let people know we are Mormons, as nicely as we can, we are better for it. People respect us for our beliefs. They might not agree with us, but they respect us, as we respect them and their beliefs.

I guess there was a time when Mormons were not as well known—when the word was spoken in a whisper as if we were witches of sorts, or horned beasts. That day is past in most of the world—or at least in the wiser parts of it. We are respected for our principles. We are admired—if we merit that admiration.

And I have learned that example means so much in each situation. I joined the Church partly because of examples set by Mormons I knew. I want to do as much for others as they did for me.

Besides, I just thoroughly enjoy being a Mormon.

Hack Miller, *The New Billy Casper* (Salt Lake City: Deseret Book Co., 1968), pp. 132-35.

SUSA YOUNG GATES*

"Whence Came the Light"

The early days of April in the year 1893 were heavy with storm and gloom. A leaden sky stretched over the earth; every day the rain beat down upon it, and the storm-winds swept over it with terrific force. Yet the brightness and the glory of those days far outshone the gloom. It was during those tempestuous days of early April that the Salt Lake Temple was dedicated.

During the dedicatory services, it was my privilege to transcribe the official notes of the various meetings. At the first service, which was known as the "official dedication," I was sitting on the lower side of the east pulpits, at the recorder's table. Brother John Nicholson, who had been busy at the outer gate, came in and sat down beside me. Just as President Joseph F. Smith began to address the Saints, there shone through his

---

*Susa Young Gates was born March 18, 1856, in Salt Lake City, a daughter of Brigham Young and Lucy Bigelow. In 1880 she was married to Jacob Gates. The mother of 13 children, she was editor and founder of the *Young Woman's Journal*, and later served as editor of the *Relief Society Magazine*. The author of textbooks on genealogy, homemaking, and other subjects, she served on the Relief Society general board from 1911 to 1922. She died on May 27, 1933, in Salt Lake City.

countenance a radiant light that gave me a peculiar feeling. I thought that the clouds must have lifted, and that a stream of sunlight had lighted on the President's head.

I turned to Brother Nicholson and whispered: "What a singular effect of sunlight on the face of President Smith! Do look at it."

He whispered back: "There is no sunlight outdoors—nothing but dark clouds and gloom."

I looked out of the window, and somewhat to my surprise, I saw that Brother Nicholson had spoken the truth. There was not the slightest rift in the heavy, black clouds above the city; there was not a gleam of sunshine anywhere.

Whence, then, came the light that shone from the face of President Smith? I was sure that I had seen the actual presence of the Holy Spirit, focused upon the features of the beloved leader and prophet, Joseph F. Smith. It was but an added testimony to me that he was the "Chosen of the Lord." I cherish the occurrence as one of the most sacred experiences of my life.

Preston Nibley, *Faith-Promoting Stories* (Independence, Missouri: Zion's Printing and Publishing Company, 1943), pp. 47-48.

Biographical Sketch

RACHEL IVINS GRANT

Rachel Ivins Grant was born March 7, 1821, at Hornerstown, New Jersey, a daughter of Caleb and Edith Ridgway Ivins. Her father died when she was six years old, and her mother died three years later.

As a young lady she was converted to The Church of Jesus Christ of Latter-day Saints. It was while she was living with her grandfather that she heard of some strangers called "Mormons" who had come to their neighborhood. She soon handed in her name for baptism and rendered willing obedience to the requirements of the gospel of Jesus Christ as revealed through the Prophet Joseph.

She traveled to Utah in 1853. Two years later she married Jedediah Morgan Grant, a counselor to President Brigham Young. One of the neighbors remarked: "Brother Grant has married a queen." She had one child, a son, Heber Jeddy Grant, who was born just nine days before her husband's untimely death. He became the seventh President of the Church.

She supported her son by sewing and keeping boarders. For thirty-five years she served as president of the Relief Society of the Thirteenth Ward in Salt Lake City. She died on January 27, 1909, at the home of her granddaughter in Salt Lake City.

RACHEL IVINS GRANT

"A New Light Seemed to Break Upon Me"

My grandparents on both sides were Quakers; consequently I was brought up under that influence. But the silent worship of the Friends did not satisfy the cravings of my soul. I longed to hear the beautiful hymns that my mother taught to her little children even in our tender years, and the spirit often moved me to burst out in songs of praise, and it was with difficulty that I could refrain from doing so.

At the age of sixteen years, with the consent of my relatives, I joined the Baptist Church. The singing pleased me and the prayers were somewhat inspiring, but the sermons were not much more satisfactory than the none-at-all of the Quakers. I was religiously inclined but not of the long-faced variety. I thought religion ought to make people happier, and that was the kind of religion I was looking for.

About this time we heard of some strange preachers called "Mormons" who had come to our neighborhood. I concluded they were some of the false prophets that the Bible speaks of, and I had no desire to see or hear them. . . .

I went to the meeting on Saturday, but when asked to go

on Sunday I did not know whether I ought to break the Sabbath day by going to hear them or not. But I finally went. Upon returning home I went to my room, knelt down, and asked the Lord to forgive me for thus breaking the Sabbath day.

I attended some more meetings and commenced reading the Book of Mormon, "Voice of Warning," and other works, and was soon convinced that they were true. A new light seemed to break upon me. The scriptures were plainer to my mind, and the light of the everlasting gospel began to illumine my soul.

While I was thus investigating, a little child died whose mother had joined the Latter-day Saints. The Baptist minister took occasion to refer to the death of the little one, regretting that its parents had neglected to have it baptized, and that thereby it was lost and could not have salvation. I afterwards heard Elder Orson Hyde preach the funeral sermon. He portrayed the glories of our Father's kingdom and the saved condition of the little innocent ones who died before they came to years of accountability—"For of such is the kingdom of heaven."

The contrast was very great, showing one to be false and the other true. I was steadily being drawn to the gospel net.

One day while I was attending the Baptist prayer meeting, our pastor admonished me for the course I was taking and said if I did not stop going to the Mormon meetings, I could not hold my seat in the Baptist Church, and they would be obliged to disfellowship me for listening to false doctrines.

This seemed to settle the question with me. One wanted to hold me against my convictions, and the other was free salvation, without money and without price.

I soon handed in my name for baptism and rendered willing obedience to the first four requirements of the gospel of Jesus Christ as revealed through the Prophet Joseph in the last dispensation of the fulness of times. And oh, what joy filled my being! I could sing all the day long and rejoice in the glorious promises of the gospel.

Relief Society Magazine, April 1943, pp. 228-29.

"He Was Always So Jolly"

I was many times at the Prophet's [Joseph Smith's] home. We used to have parties there. But not so many times when I saw him. He was a fine, noble looking man. Always so neat. When he was preaching you could feel the influence and power. He was not at home very much. There were so few that he could trust or put confidence in. His life was so often sought that he had to be hid up. After he had been in hiding and had come out he was always so jolly and happy. He was different in that respect from Brother Hyrum, who was more sedate, more serious.

Relief Society Magazine, April 1943, p. 229.

RACHEL IVINS GRANT

"The Latchstring Will Be Out"

As told by Heber J. Grant

At the age of sixteen mother joined the Baptist Church, with the consent of her relatives. Sometime later, while she was visiting at the home of an uncle in Hornerstown, New Jersey, she went to a meeting at which the Mormon missionaries were preaching. Subsequently she met the minister of the Baptist church in which she had a pew, and he said:

"Miss Ivins, you went to hear those awful Mormons. If you go to hear them again your pew in my church will be vacant."

I have understood that there is no one on earth so stubborn as a Scotsman, except a Dutchman, and my father was Scot and my mother Dutch. What the minister said to my mother got her "Dutch" up, and she said to him: "My pew is vacant in your church. I shall go to hear these Mormons, and I shall pray. It may be that they have the truth."

She told me that when she attended the first Latter-day Saint meeting, she only went out of curiosity and did not listen attentively or prayerfully, but went merely to please her sister and one of her girl friends. That was on a Saturday. The night after attending her first Mormon meeting on a Sunday she got down on her knees and prayed the Lord to forgive her for doing such a wicked thing as going to listen to false prophets on the Sabbath.

But she became converted to the restored gospel. The men who converted her were the Prophet Joseph Smith himself and Erastus Snow. And my mother's brothers who were well-to-do financially offered to settle an annuity upon her for life if she would renounce her religion. One of her brothers said to her: "Rachel, you have disgraced the name of Ivins. We never want to see you again if you stay with those awful Mormons,"—this was when she was leaving for Utah—"but," he continued, "come back in a year, come back in five years, come back in ten or twenty years, and no matter when you come back, the latchstring will be out, and affluence and ease will be your portion."

Later, when poverty became her lot, if she actually had not known that Joseph Smith was a prophet of God and that the gospel was true, all she needed to have done was to return east and let her brothers take care of her. But rather than return to her wealthy relatives in the East where she would have been amply provided for, with no struggle for herself or her child, she preferred to make her way among those to whom she was more strongly attached than her kindred who were not believers in her faith. And so she sewed, at first by hand with a needle and thread and later with a sewing machine, and kept boarders to make· a living for herself and her little child. Although she had

21

been reared in affluence, she adapted herself to conditions of poverty, and her home was always a pattern of neatness.

Improvement Era, May 1936, pp. 267-68.

RACHEL   IVINS   GRANT

"Behave Yourself, Heber"

For years, Heber J. Grant's mother cherished in her heart promises that were made to her son in childhood. She had implicit faith in the fulfillment of those promises, provided he lived worthy of them. Referring to his mother, President Grant said: "My mother always told me, 'Behave yourself, Heber, and some day you will be an apostle. If you do not behave yourself, you will not be, because we have a revelation recorded in the Doctrine and Covenants which specifically states, 'There is a law irrevocably decreed in heaven before the foundations of the world upon which all blessings are predicated, and when we obtain any blessing from God, it is by obedience to that law upon which it is predicated.' [D&C 130: 20.] I said, 'Mother, I do not want to be an apostle. I do not want to be a bishop. I do not want to be anything but a businessman. Just get it out of your head.' "

When he was called to the apostleship, she asked him if he remembered a meeting where certain blessings were promised him. He replied: "No, I do not remember anything, only that when Aunt Zina was talking she said, 'You will become a great man in The Church of Jesus Christ of Latter-day Saints and one of the apostles of the Lord Jesus Christ.' "

22

His mother said: "That is the reason I have told you to behave yourself. I knew it would not come true if you did not live worthily, but it has come true." Then she asked, "Do you remember Heber C. Kimball picking you up when you were a young boy and putting you on a table and talking to you at a great dinner he was having for a lot of his friends?"

"Yes."

"Do you remember anything that he said?"

"No, I only remember that he had the blackest eyes I have ever looked into. I was frightened. That is all I can remember."

"He prophesied in the name of the Lord Jesus Christ that you would become an apostle of the Lord Jesus Christ and become a greater man in the Church than your own father; and your father, as you know, became one of the counselors to President Brigham Young. That is why I have told you to behave."

Bryant S. Hinckley, *The Faith of Our Pioneer Fathers* (Salt Lake City: Deseret Book Co., 1956), pp. 69-71.

RACHEL   IVINS   GRANT

"He Was Very Sorry for Widow Grant"

As told by Heber J. Grant

Referring to that wonderful mother of mine, I remembered that one day we had at least a half-dozen, if not more, buckets on the floor catching the rain that came from the roof. It was raining very heavily, and Bishop Edwin D. Woolley came into the house and said, "Why, Widow Grant, this will never do. I shall take some of the money from the fast offering and put a new roof on this house."

"Oh, no, you won't," said Mother. "No relief money will ever put a roof on my house. I have sewing here, and I have supported myself and my son with a needle and thread for many years and later with a Wheeler and Wilcox sewing machine." . . .

Then Mother said, "When I get through with this sewing that I'm doing now, I will buy some shingles and patch the holes in the roof, and this house will take care of me until my son gets to be a man and builds me a new one."

Bishop Woolley went away and said he was very sorry for Widow Grant and that if she waited for that boy to build a house she would never have one, for he was the laziest boy in the whole Thirteenth Ward. He went on to tell how I wasted my time throwing a ball across the fence behind the house hour after hour, day after day, and week after week at his adobe barn. Thank the Lord for a mother who was a general as well as a Latter-day Saint, who realized that it is a remarkable and splendid thing to encourage a boy to do something besides, perhaps, milking cows if he was on a farm, or encourage him if he had ambitions along athletic lines.

Bryant S. Hinckley, *Heber J. Grant, Highlights in the Life of a Great Leader* (Salt Lake City: Deseret Book Co., 1951), pp. 38-39.

RACHEL   IVINS   GRANT

"Mother, I Don't Want a Naval Education"

As told by Heber J. Grant

I met President George Q. Cannon, then our delegate to Congress, and he said: "Would you like to go to the Naval Academy or to West Point?"

I told him I would.

He said: "Which one?"

I said, "The Naval Academy."

"All right, I will give you the appointment without competitive examination."

For the first time in my life I did not sleep well; I lay awake nearly all night long rejoicing that the ambition of my life was to be fulfilled. I fell asleep just a little before daylight; my mother had to awaken me.

I said: "Mother, what a marvelous thing it is that I am to have an education as fine as that of any young man in all Utah. I could hardly sleep; I was awake until almost daylight this morning."

I looked into her face; I saw that she had been weeping.

I have heard of people who, when drowning, had their entire life pass before them in a few seconds. I saw myself an admiral, in my mind's eye. I saw myself traveling all over the world in a ship, away from my widowed mother. I laughed and put my arms around her and kissed her and said, "Mother, I do not want a naval education. I am going to be a businessman and shall enter an office right away and take care of you and have you quit keeping boarders for a living."

She broke down and wept and said that she had not closed her eyes, but had prayed all night that I would give up my life's ambition so that she would not be left alone.

Her prayers were answered, and her appeal to the Almighty was inspired by promises made to her son in his childhood by those she looked upon as being the servants of God.

Hinckley, *Heber J. Grant*, pp. 33-34.

JANE GROVER

*"I Talked to Those Indians
in Their Own Language"*

One morning we thought we
would go and gather gooseberries. Father Tanner, as we familiarly called the good, patriarchal Elder Nathan Tanner, harnessed
a span of horses to a light wagon and, with two sisters by the
name of Lyman, his little granddaughter, and me, started out.
When we reached the woods we told the old gentleman to go to
a house in sight and rest himself while we picked the berries.

It was not long before the little girl and I strayed some distance from the rest, when suddenly we heard shouts. The little
girl thought it was her grandfather and was about to answer, but
I restrained her, thinking it might be Indians. We walked forward until within sight of Father Tanner, when we saw he was
running his team around. We thought nothing strange at first,
but as we approached we saw Indians gathering around the
wagon, whooping and yelling as others came and joined them.
We got into the wagon to start when four of the Indians took
hold of the wagon wheels to stop the wagon, and two others held
the horses by the bits, and another came to take me out of the
wagon.

I then began to be afraid as well as vexed, and asked Father Tanner to let me get out of the wagon and run for assistance. He said, "No poor child; it is too late!" I told him they should not take me alive. His face was as white as a sheet. The Indians had commenced to strip him—had taken his watch and handkerchief —and while stripping him, were trying to pull me out of the wagon. I began silently to appeal to my Heavenly Father.

While I was praying and struggling, the Spirit of the Almighty fell upon me and I arose with great power; and no tongue can tell my feelings. I was happy as I could be. A few moments before I saw worse than death staring me in the face, and now my hand was raised by the power of God, and I talked to those Indians in their own language. They let go the horses and wagon, and all stood in front of me while I talked to them by the power of God. They bowed their heads and answered "Yes," in a way that made me know what they meant.

The little girl and Father Tanner looked on in speechless amazement. I realized our situation; their calculation was to kill Father Tanner, burn the wagon, and take us women prisoners. This was plainly shown me. When I stopped talking they shook hands with all three of us and returned all they had taken from Father Tanner, who gave them back the handkerchief, and I gave them berries and crackers. By this time the other two women came up, and we hastened home.

The Lord gave me a portion of the interpretation of what I had said, which was as follows:

"I suppose you Indian warriors think you are going to kill us? Don't you know the Great Spirit is watching you and knows everything in your heart? We have come out here to gather some of our father's fruit. We have not come to injure you; and if you harm us, or injure one hair of our heads, the Great Spirit shall smite you to the earth, and you shall not have power to breathe another breath. We have been driven from our homes, and so have you; we have come out here to do you good, and not to injure you. We are the Lord's people and so are you; but you must cease your murders and wickedness; the Lord is displeased with it and will not prosper you if you continue in it. You think you own all this land, this timber, this water, all the horses.

Why, you do not own one thing on earth, not even the air you breath—it all belongs to the Great Spirit."

Edward Tullidge, *The Women of Mormondom*, pp. 475-77.

MARY ANN HAFEN*

"Father Turned Away and Wiped Tears From His Eyes"

Our company was organized with Oscar O. Stoddard as captain. It contained 126 persons with twenty-two handcarts and three provision wagons drawn by oxen. We set out from Florence on July 6, 1860, for our thousand-mile trip. There were six to our cart. Father and Mother pulled it; Rosie (two years old) and Christian (six months old) rode; John (nine) and I (six) walked. Sometimes, when it was downhill, they let me ride too.

The first night out the mosquitoes gave us a hearty welcome. Father had brought a cow along, so we could have milk on the way. At first he tied her to the back of the cart, but she would sometimes hang back, so he thought he would make a harness and have her pull the cart while he led her. By this time Mother's feet were so swollen that she could not wear shoes, but had to wrap her feet with cloth. Father thought that by having the cow pull the cart Mother might ride. This worked well for some time.

*Mary Ann Stucki Hafen was born on May 5, 1854, at Rotenback, Switzerland. Her parents joined the Church and emigrated to Utah, crossing the plains with the tenth and last handcart company, in 1860. She married John George Hafen on November 24, 1873, and had seven children. They pioneered in Utah and southern Nevada.

One day a group of Indians came riding up on horses. Their jingling trinkets, dragging poles, and strange appearance frightened the cow and sent her chasing off with the cart and children. We were afraid that the children might be killed, but the cow fell into a deep gully and the cart turned upside down. Although the children were under the trunk and bedding, they were unhurt, but after that Father did not hitch the cow to the cart again. He let three Danish boys take her to hitch to their cart. Then the Danish boys, each in turn, would help Father pull our cart.

Of course we had many other difficulties. One was that it was hard for the carts to keep up with the three provision wagons drawn by ox teams. Often the men pulling the carts would try to take shortcuts through the brush and sand in order to keep up.

After about three weeks my mother's feet became better, so she could wear her shoes again. She would get so discouraged and down-hearted; but Father never lost courage. He would always cheer her up by telling her that we were going to Zion, that the Lord would take care of us, and that better times were coming.

Even when it rained the company did not stop traveling. A cover on the handcart shielded the two younger children. The rest of us found it more comfortable moving than standing still in the drizzle. In fording streams, the men often carried the children and weaker women across on their backs. The company stopped over on Sundays for rest, and meetings were held for spiritual comfort and guidance. At night, when the handcarts were drawn up in a circle and the fires were lighted, the camp looked quite happy. Singing, music, and speeches by the leaders cheered everyone. I remember that we stopped one night at an old Indian campground. There were many bright-colored beads in the ant hills.

At times we met or were passed by the overland stage coach with its passengers and mail bags and drawn by four fine horses. When the Pony Express dashed past, it seemed almost like the wind racing over the prairie.

Our provisions began to get low. One day a herd of buffalo

ran past and the men of our company shot two of them. Such a feast as we had when they were dressed! Each family was given a piece of meat to take along. My brother John, who pushed at the back of our cart, used to tell how hungry he was all the time and how tired he got from pushing. He said he felt that if he could just sit down for a few minutes, he would feel so much better. But instead, Father would ask if he couldn't push a little harder. Mother was nursing the baby and could not help much, especially when the food ran short and she grew weak. When rations were reduced, Father gave Mother a part of his share of the food, so he was not so strong either.

When we got that chunk of buffalo meat, Father put it in the handcart. My brother John remembered that it was the fore part of the week and that Father said we would save it for Sunday dinner. John said, "I was so very hungry and the meat smelled so good to me while pushing at the handcart that I could not resist. I had a little pocket knife and with it I cut off a piece or two each half day. Although I expected a severe whipping when Father found it out, I cut off little pieces each day. I would chew them so long that they got white and perfectly tasteless. When Father came to get the meat he asked me if I had been cutting off some of it. I said, 'Yes, I was so hungry I could not let it alone.' Instead of giving me a scolding or whipping, Father turned away and wiped tears from his eyes."

Even when we were on short rations, if we met a band of Indians the captain of our company would give them some of the provisions so the Indians would let us go by in safety. Food finally became so low that word was sent to Salt Lake City, and in about two weeks fresh supplies arrived.

At last, when we reached the top of Emigration Canyon, overlooking Salt Lake, on that September day, 1860, the whole company stopped to look down through the valley. Some yelled and tossed their hats in the air. A shout of joy arose at the thought that our long trip was over, that we had at last reached Zion, the place of rest. We all gave thanks to God for helping us safely over the plains and mountains to our destination.

When we arrived in the city we were welcomed by the people, who came out carrying baskets of fruit and other kinds of good things to eat. Even though we could not understand their language, they made us feel that we were among friends.

We were invited home by a good family who kept us two or three days, until my parents were rested. Then we were given a little house near the river Jordan, three miles from town, and Father was put to work on the public road. He was paid in produce, mostly flour and potatoes, from the Tithing Office.

Mary Ann Hafen, *Recollections of a Handcart Pioneer of 1860* (Denver, Colorado: privately printed, 1938), pp. 22-27.

Biographical Sketch

DARYL V. HOOLE

Daryl V. Hoole has become well-known throughout the Church for her teachings and writings on homemaking and family living. This all came about shortly after her marriage in 1957 when spontaneous requests from neighbors and friends came to her concerning how she so easily and effectively managed her home. These queries caused her to closely examine her habits as a homemaker and to try to offer constructive help to these discouraged women.

It came as a surprise to her that not all women with homes knew how to keep them. Daryl, the eldest of four children of Donovan H. and Ada S. Van Dam, had grown up in a home where good habits, orderliness, and organization made it a smooth-running, happy place.

Her father, a reserve army officer, was called to active duty during World War II. The family left their Salt Lake City home and spent seven years moving from one army camp to another. Thus, Daryl attended eighteen different schools—six first grades —before she was graduated from high school. Undoubtedly all of those moves were helpful in teaching her the value of organized, yet flexible living.

At the close of the war, the Van Dam family returned to Salt Lake City to once more establish their home, but they were again called away in 1952, this time to Europe where Brother Van Dam was to preside over the Netherlands Mission. Daryl left with her family during her senior year in high school and shortly after her arrival in Holland was called and set apart as a full-time missionary. In addition to fulfilling a mission and learning the Dutch language, Daryl traveled extensively throughout Europe and attended the dedication of the Swiss Temple.

She was married to H. J. M. (Hank) Hoole, Jr., in the Salt Lake Temple on March 25, 1957. They have had nine children, eight of whom are living.

Daryl has served in Church auxiliary organizations and is currently Spiritual Living leader in the Yalecrest Second Ward Relief Society in Salt Lake City. Her husband is first counselor in the bishopric of that ward.

Daryl Hoole's book *The Art of Homemaking* has become an LDS best-seller and has been widely used and praised. It has made the term "Let's do it according to Hoole" a household phrase in countless homes.

Another book, *The Art of Teaching Children*, has also been well received; she collaborated with her sister, Mrs. Gail W. Ockey (Donette), in this project.

Daryl Hoole teaches and lectures throughout the Church and has helped women perpetuate the spirit of her classes by making a live recording entitled "Seven to Eleven Can Be Heaven." She has also written a number of articles that have appeared in Church magazines.

DARYL V. HOOLE

"No Two Diamonds Are Alike"

Ella struggled to hold back her tears as she ran along the stone walk to Aunt Susan's apartment at the rear of her home. As Ella rushed up to her aunt, the tears, which had been too near the surface too much of the time lately, spilled over. "Oh, Aunt Susan," sobbed Ella, "nobody likes me. I'm just no good. I wish I weren't such a dumb—" More sobs blotted out the rest of her words. . . .

Aunt Susan had laid her knitting aside and was waiting for her young niece to go on with her problem. "Why do you feel that no one likes you? What makes you think you're dumb and no good?" she encouraged.

"It's just terrible, Aunt Susan, to live with Bevie and Ruth. They make me feel awful. Bevie is so friendly with everyone and can always find so much to talk about. Everybody just loves her. Almost every phone call at our house is for her. She gets invited to all the parties and has all the fun. Whenever I'm in a group of people, I either say the wrong thing or . . . or else I can't think of anything to say at all. Bevie isn't afraid to talk to anyone, and she's so clever and full of fun. Oh, I wish I could be like Bevie.

"And Ruth makes me feel so dumb and stupid. She can do

anything. Mother and Daddy are forever bragging about her accomplishments. I never do anything worth mentioning. It seems all I hear around our house is talk about her scholarship from the university or how the new three-piece suit she just made is so beautiful or something else she has done. Even the bishop said the other day that when Ruth goes away to school he doesn't know what he'll do for a Sunday School organist. She's always in demand for her piano playing. Everyone says things like: 'There's just no one quite like Ruth,' or 'She's the most talented and capable girl I've ever seen.' It goes on and on, and the more she does, the dumber I feel."

Aunt Susan thought for a long time before responding to Ella. Finally she said, "I can understand how you feel, Ella. It would be difficult to live with two very popular, talented older sisters. It could make you feel quite inferior. I would like to make three suggestions to you. You might like to write them down and read them often—even memorize them—so that you'll remember them for the rest of your life.

"First, you're comparing yourself with someone else. This is unfair. You're much younger than your sisters. Bevie has had several years more practice talking with people and learning to express herself well and saying clever things. I feel sure you'll gain in confidence and will feel you have more to contribute to conversations as you grow older. Time has done a lot for Ruth, too. As I think back to her piano playing when she was your age, it sounded just the way yours does. Who's to say what accomplishments will be yours by the time you graduate from high school? You've been busy laying your foundation for life these past thirteen years. It's just about now that you can start to build on that foundation and really do things. It's all wrong to compare yourself with others, Ella. The only real basis for comparison is within yourself. Don't feel bad if your piano playing—or anything else—isn't as good as Ruth's. Just make certain that you play better now than you did a year ago. It's wonderful to have people such as Ruth inspire you to do better and reach loftier goals, but compete with yourself—not someone else!

"Now the second thing I want you to remember always is this: That which someone else does needn't detract from that which you do. Just because Bevie has lots of friends doesn't mean that you have any fewer friends of your own. Just because someone has beautiful eyes doesn't mean that your eyes are ugly. Nothing Ruth knows or does or has need detract from what you know or do or have.

"And third and most important, Ella, our Father in heaven has taken great care to create each one of us individually. Don't try to make yourself like someone else. Be grateful for your own talents and gifts and do your best to cultivate them. Why, it was just last week at Relief Society I heard several mothers discussing baby sitters. They mentioned your name and said how confident they feel when you are with their children and how much their children enjoy you. Sister Astin said that because of your conscientiousness toward responsibility and your ability to handle children exceptionally well, you make an ideal baby sitter.

"I've heard your mother say on many occasions how she depends on you to help her. She says you always do your work well and willingly and do so much to make your home a better place to be.

"Have you ever realized, Ella, that when someone is ill, you know just what to do to bring the most comfort? I recall my bout with rheumatism last winter . . . it was you who took the time to run my errands, keep fresh flowers by my bedside, and cheer me through your visits. You have a fine mind, Ella. I've observed that you have a quest for knowledge. You love school and do very well there. I could go on, Ella, for you have many gifts and talents that make you special just the way you are. I read something last week I want to share with you. I hope it will impress you as it did me. Did you know that no two diamonds are, or ever have been, alike? This diamond I am wearing on my finger is unlike any other diamond on earth. That's one of the reasons the diamond has become, since ancient times, the gem of kings and emperors and holds the greatest value of all worldly possessions. No two diamonds are alike, but they are all jewels. Never forget that you are a jewel, Ella."

Ella's heart felt lighter than ever before.

Daryl V. Hoole and Donette V. Ockey, *With Sugar and Spice* (Salt Lake City: Deseret Book Co., 1966), pp. 19-21.

DARYL   V.   HOOLE

"Time to Create Harmony"

The following story was told to Sister Hoole

My grandmother had eleven children, and it seemed as if there was always harmony in her family. I asked my mother one day if she could remember anything specific that might help me to be like her. She said that the incident she remembered best was one time when her brothers, who were supposed to be sawing wood, were quarreling. She recalled that her mother was hurrying to prepare a dinner for Church officials, but she stopped and went out and sat on a block of wood near where the boys were sawing, and said the magic words, "Let me tell you a story." My mother said she didn't hear the story, but soon saw her brothers and mother laughing. Later when she went inside, the boys resumed their work without any thought of what they had been quarreling about.

The thought I gleaned from this incident was that my grandmother and mother, too, always took the time to create the harmony that was in our homes. They always had the time to listen to our thoughts, to tell us a story, always to be conscious of our needs.

Daryl V. Hoole, *The Art of Teaching Children* (Salt Lake City: Deseret Book Co., 1972), pp. 21-22.

"A School Reader Open in the Bed"

One morning my small son said to me at breakfast, "Daddy, may I read to you? I got nine out of ten for reading at school yesterday."

"Very good," said I, hardly glancing from my paper.

"May I?"

"Eh? May you what?" I demanded—being in haste, and wishful to glance over the news and finish breakfast in next to no time.

"May I read to you?"

"Well, not now, son! There's no time!"

So off I went to catch a bus.

Home that evening, I told my little son that I would listen to his reading as soon as I had had my supper. But somebody called, and I had to see him. And then somebody else called, and I had to engage him. And finally I went into my son's bedroom, and found him fast asleep, his cheeks wet with tears, a school reader open on the bed.

Thus, through this experience, I learned my lesson: to love him a little more and myself a little less.

The Art of Teaching Children, p. 34.

"Gospel Study and Knowledge"

Our teaching methods must develop as a child develops and keep pace with his understanding. A lesson that is challenging to an eight-year-old will seem dull and silly to a teenager. The lessons must progress with the intellectual maturity of a child so he won't ever reach a point where they seem childish and foolish.

A brilliant young member of the Church announced his plans to study for a doctor's degree in philosophy. Some of his friends and family members foresaw the loss of his testimony and his falling away from the Church. He assured them this would not happen and stated his plans to study the gospel right along with philosophy, which he did.

During the years of his graduate work, he also completed an extensive study of the Doctrine and Covenants. As he was graduated with a Ph.D., he also had a stronger testimony than ever of the divinity of the Church and the truthfulness of the gospel. He is a great spiritual leader and among other assignments has served the Church well as a mission president.

Some people get a doctor's degree from a university but have only a third-grade understanding of the gospel. Gospel study and knowledge must keep pace with academic study and knowledge.

As has been pointed out, teaching your children the gospel effectively will take time, effort, and study. But if you really want to, you will find the time by planning for it, working for it, and taking it, and will put forth the necessary effort and study.

> To have sown in the souls of men
> One thought that will not die—
> To have been a link in the chain of life
> Shall be immortality.

Hoole, *The Art of Teaching Children.* p. 105-106.

"It Could Revolutionize Your Life"

Charles Schwab, one of the first presidents of Bethlehem Steel Company, once inquired of efficiency expert Ivy Lee: "If you can give us something to pep us up to do the things we know we ought to do, I'll gladly pay you anything within reason you ask."

"Fine," answered Lee. "I can give you something in two minutes that will step up your 'doing' by at least fifty percent."

"All right," said Mr. Schwab. "Let's have it."

Mr. Lee handed Mr. Schwab a blank sheet of note paper and said: "Write down the six most important tasks you have to do tomorrow and number them in the order of their importance. Now, put this paper in your pocket and the first thing tomorrow morning look at item one and start working on it until it is finished. Then tackle item two in the same way; then item three and so on. Do this until quitting time.

"Don't be concerned if you have only finished one or two. You'll be working on the most important ones. The others can wait. If you can't finish them all by this method, you couldn't have with any other method either; and without some system, you'd probably not even have decided which was the most important.

"Do this every working day. After you've convinced yourself of the value of this system, have your men try it. Try it as long as you wish and then send me a check for what you think it is worth."

A few weeks later Mr. Schwab sent Ivy Lee a check for $25,000 with a letter saying the lesson was the most profitable he had ever learned.

In five years, this plan was largely responsible for turning the unknown Bethlehem Steel Company into the biggest independent

steel producer in the world. And it helped to make Charles
Schwab one hundred million dollars.

This can work for you! Try it! It could revolutionize your
life.

_____

Daryl V. Hoole, *The Art of Homemaking* (Salt Lake City: Deseret Book Co.,
1967), pp. 90-91.

MARY ISABELLA HORNE*

"I Made Cornstalk Molasses in My Wash Boiler"

We arrived in Salt Lake Valley in the evening of October 6, 1847. From the mouth of the canyon we traveled in the dark, having no guide, but the flickering light of the campfires on Pioneer Square. Our tent was soon pitched, and we felt thankful to our Heavenly Father for preserving us on our long and arduous journey of four months, and that we had arrived at a place of rest. We lived in a tent until logs could be obtained from the canyon for a house.

It must be remembered that at that early day there were no sawmills; the saw-pits were the only means of obtaining lumber. These were made by digging a trench ten feet long and five feet deep, above which trestles were built. The log to be sawed was laid on these trestles. One man stood on the top of the log

*Mary Isabella Horne was born November 20, 1880, at Raeriham, Kent, England, a daughter of Stephen and Mary Ann Hales. At the age of 14 she immigrated to America. She was married to Joseph Horne on May 9, 1836; they were converted to The Church of Jesus Christ of Latter-day Saints two months later. Active in the Church auxiliaries, Mrs. Horne was one of the first members of the Young Ladies Retrenchment Association (YWMIA) and was placed in charge of the adult department. She also served on the Relief Society general board and the Deseret Hospital board. She died August 27, 1906.

and another in the pit, and they pulled the saw up and down. You can readily imagine that with this slow process it was a long time before we could have board floors in our houses.

When we moved into our little two-room house there were neither floors nor doors. We had brought two small windows with us. Of course we had no furniture, so we had to manufacture some the best we could. Our bedstead was made in one corner of the room by boring holes in the logs of the house about six feet from the corner on one side, four feet on the other and two feet from the floor, into which the ends of poles were inserted, the other ends being fastened to a post set in the ground. Wooden pegs were driven in these poles and the logs of the house at regular intervals, on which strips of rawhide were stretched, crossing from side to side and head to foot. This formed quite a comfortable spring mattress, upon which the bedding was placed.

Our cupboard was made by placing a large packing box on its side upon some brackets made by fastening short poles in the wall. Shelves were put in, and these as well as other packing boxes which were brought into use as toilet table, etc., were draped with calico curtains. Tables and stools were formed from poles and boxes. These with the little wooden rocker and cook stove completed our house furnishings.

Our candle was a little grease in a saucer with a twisted rag in it. I put some lamp black and yellow ochre into a little skim milk I obtained from a neighbor, and stained our door and window frames, using a rag for a brush, which made them look more homelike and saved considerable scrubbing.

We had succeeded in arranging things quite comfortably when a cloud burst up City Creek Canyon and the water came rushing down, covering our floor an inch or two deep. Our provisions were our first care. They must be kept dry and used sparingly. Our rations were weighed out for a week, so much and no more.

Segoes and wild parsnips were gathered and used as food. We did not have milk; members of the company had lost some of their oxen while crossing the plains, and our cows had been used in their place. Graham gruel without milk or sugar was used for breakfast and supper.

The weather continued fine until March 1848, when a storm came on and we had rain, snow, and sleet continually for ten days. Our house being covered only with poles, grass, and earth, it continued to rain in the house after it was fine outside. Wagon covers were fastened nearly to the roof over the head of the bed, sloping to the foot to shed the water and keep the bed dry. A large piece of table oil cloth was tacked up over the table while we ate our meals, and it was no uncommon thing to see a woman holding an umbrella over her while attending to her household duties. The fort presented quite a ludicrous appearance when the weather cleared up. In whatever direction one looked, bedding and clothing of all descriptions were hanging out to dry.

One of the greatest sources of trouble and inconvenience was the mice. The ground was full of them. They ran over us in our beds, ate into our boxes, and destroyed much valuable clothing. Various kinds of mousetraps were devised, but relief was obtained only after securing a kitten from the only family of cats in the camp.

Early in the spring a man came into the valley from California with some pack animals, and brought some potatoes. Mr. Horne paid him fifty cents for four potatoes about as large as a hen's egg, from which he raised over a bushel of fine potatoes. But we could not eat them. They must be saved for seed. During that year quite a variety of good vegetables was raised. The melons, pumpkin, and squash were very sweet. I made cornstalk molasses in my wash boiler, also melon preserves and pumpkin sauce by boiling the juice of the melons to syrup and thickening with squash or pumpkin. We had beets, turnips, carrots, and onions in the garden, and as we had been without vegetables for nearly three years, I thought I had never eaten anything so good. Our sugar was all gone, but about this time a man brought some in from California. I had waited with others for an hour and a half to get into the house where it was, and then could only have one pound of brown sugar, for which I paid one dollar.

Nibley, *Faith-Promoting Stories*, pp. 67-70.

CATHERINE CHRISTINA
JENSEN *

"You Just Dreamed It"

Catherine Christina Jensen crossed the plains with a handcart company during the summer of 1857. During their travels they, by mistake, left the road and were lost for a day and a night. At this time they were without water. When evening came all were tired, worn out, and thirsty. As they retired for night, prayers were offered, asking God to help them find their way and to find water before conditions became too serious.

. . . being a very faithful woman, and in a delicate condition, she was too thirsty to sleep. She began crying and prayed silently to her Heavenly Father, asking him to send water to them. While all the camp was quiet . . . she thought she heard water. At first she thought it was her imagination, but soon she realized it was really water. She quietly crept from her bed and followed the sound. Sure enough, she found a small, clear, cold stream was running close to their camp. She drank all the

*Catherine Christina Jensen, who was born on December 5, 1832, was the wife of Nels Ceron Jensen and the mother of one child. This story was written by her granddaughter, Alla Loveland, who stated that throughout her life her grandmother looked on this incident as an answer to prayer.

water she could, then went back to camp and woke her husband. As she told him of the water, he said, "Catherine, you just dreamed it because you are suffering for water." But he finally consented to go with her to the place. He then rushed back to the camp and told the men. They watered their oxen, filled their vessels, and went back to bed. The next morning the stream had dried away.

Carter, *Heart Throbs of the West,* vol. 3, pp. 337.

ELIZABETH
JACKSON KINGSFORD *

"My Husband Was Dead"

Elizabeth Jackson Kingsford de-
scribes the journey across the plains as a long and tedious one.
We continued our toil day after day, *she writes,* pulling our
handcarts with our provisions and rations, our little children,
etc., through deep sand, rocky roads, or fording streams. It was a
dreary journey. Many miles each day were traveled, ere with
tired limbs we reached camp, ate and retired for the night to
rest, to pursue our monotonous course the following day. After
toilsome and fatiguing travel, we reached Laramie on the 8th
of October. . . .

Shortly after leaving Ft. Laramie it became necessary to
shorten our rations that they might hold out, and that the company be not reduced to starvation. The reduction was repeated
several times. First, the pound of flour was reduced to three-
fourths of a pound, then to half a pound, and afterwards to still

*Elizabeth Horrocks Jackson Kingsford was born August 5, 1826, at Macclesfield,
Cheshire, England, a daughter of Edward and Alice Houghton Horrocks. She was
baptized into The Church of Jesus Christ of Latter-day Saints in 1841 and was married
on May 28, 1848, to Aaron Jackson. She and her husband were members of the Edward
Martin Handcart Company; he died while crossing the plains. She was married to
William R. Kingsford in 1857. She died in Ogden, Utah, October 17, 1908.

less per day. However, we pushed ahead. The trip was full of adventures, hair breadth escapes, and exposure to attacks from Indians, wolves, and other wild beasts. When we reached the Black Hills, we had a rough experience. The roads were rocky, broken, and difficult to travel. Frequently carts were broken down and much delay caused by the needed repairs.

In crossing the Platte River some of the men carried a number of the women on their backs or in their arms across the stream. . . . We had scarcely crossed the river when we were visited with a tremendous storm of snow, hail, sand, and fierce winds. It was a terrible storm from which both the people and teams suffered. After crossing the river, my husband was unable to walk and consequently provision had to be made for him to ride in a wagon. As soon as we reached camp, I prepared some refreshments and placed him to rest for the night. From this time my worst experience commenced. The company had now become greatly reduced in strength, the teams had become so weak that the luggage was reduced to ten pounds per head for adults and five pounds per head for children under eight years. And although the weather was severe, a great deal of bedding and clothing had to be destroyed—burned—as it could not be carried along. This occurrence very much increased the suffering of the company, men, women, and children alike. On the 20th of October we traveled, or almost wallowed, for about ten miles through the snow. At night, weary and worn out, we camped near the Platte River, where we soon left it for the Sweetwater. We were visited with three days more snow. The animals and emigrants were almost completely exhausted. We remained in camp several days to gain strength.

About the 25th of October, I think it was—I cannot remember the exact date—we reached camp about sundown. My husband had for several days previous been much worse. He was still sinking, and his condition became more serious. As soon as possible, after reaching camp, I prepared a little of such scant articles of food as we then had. He tried to eat, but failed. He had not the strength to swallow. I put him to bed as quickly as I could. He seemed to rest easy and fell asleep. About 9 o'clock, I retired. Bedding had become very scarce, so I did not disrobe. I slept until, as it appeared to me, about midnight. It was extremely cold. The weather was bitter. I listened to hear if my husband breathed—he lay so still. I could not hear him. I became alarmed. I put my hand on his body when to my horror I discovered that my worst fears were confirmed. My husband was dead. He was cold and stiff—rigid in the arms of death. It was a bitter freezing night and the elements had sealed up his mortal frame. I called for help to the other inmates of the tent. They could render me no aid; and there was no alternative but to remain alone by the side of the corpse till morning. The night was enveloped in almost Egyptian darkness. There was nothing with which to produce a light or kindle a fire. Of course I could not sleep. I could only watch, wait, and pray for the dawn. But oh, how those dreary hours drew their tedious length along. When daylight came, some of the male part of the company prepared the body for burial. And oh, such burial and funeral service. They did not remove his clothing—he had but little. They wrapped him in a blanket and placed him in a pile with thirteen others who had died, and then covered him up in the snow. The ground was frozen so hard that they could not dig a grave. I will not attempt to describe my feeling at finding myself thus left a widow with three children, under such excruciating circumstances. I cannot do it. But I believe the Recording Angel has inscribed it in the archives above, and that my sufferings for the gospel's sake will be sanctified unto me for my good. . . .

A few days after the death of my husband, the male members of the company had become reduced in number by death; and those who remained were so weak and emaciated by sickness that on reaching the camping place at night, there were not sufficient men with strength enough to raise the poles and pitch the tents. The result was that we camped out with nothing but the vault of heaven for a roof and the stars for companions. The snow lay several inches deep upon the ground. The night was bitterly cold. I sat down on a rock with one child in my lap and one on each side of me. In that condition I remained until morning. . . .

It will be readily perceived that under such adverse circumstances I had become despondent. I was six or seven thousand miles from my native land, in a wild rocky mountain country, in a destitute condition, the ground covered with snow, the waters covered with ice, and I with three fatherless children with scarcely anything to protect them from the merciless storms. When I retired to bed that night, being the 27th of October, I had a stunning revelation. In my dream, my husband stood by me, and said, "Cheer up, Elizabeth, deliverance is at hand." The dream was fulfilled, for the next day (October 28, 1856) Joseph A. Young, Daniel Jones, and Abel Garr galloped unexpectedly into camp, amid tears and cheers and smiles and laughter of the emigrants. These three men were the first of the most advanced relief company sent out from Salt Lake City to meet the belated emigrants.

Andrew Jenson, *LDS Biographical Encyclopedia* (Salt Lake City: The Andrew Jenson History Co., 1901-1936), vol. 2, pp. 528-31.

LYDIA KNIGHT*

"Sister Lydia, Rise Up"

A meeting was again held, and after it was over the Prophet [Joseph Smith] baptized twelve persons, among whom [were] Lydia . . . , Mr. Nickerson, and all of his household. She who was always so sober and full of reflection had received the glad message with trembling joy. She was filled with a bright, peaceful influence and was full of gratitude that God had spared her to hear and accept his glorious gospel. . . .

So into the water goes Lydia with a light step and happy heart. She was so filled wth the Holy Ghost while standing in the water after she was baptized that she was constrained to cry aloud, "Glory to God in the highest! Thanks be to his holy name that I have lived to see this day and be a partaker of this great blessing."

°Lydia Goldthwait Knight was born June 9, 1812, in Sutton, Worcester County, Massachusetts, a daughter of Jesse Goldthwait and Sally Burt.

She became a member of the Church in 1833. Two years later, on November 23, 1835, she married Newel Knight in Kirtland, Ohio. He died in 1847, leaving Lydia on the plains with several children. One was born after his death.

After many difficulties and much suffering, the way was finally opened for Lydia Knight to continue her journey and to come to Utah. In later years she was an ordinance worker in the St. George Temple. At the time of her death, April 3, 1884, she was living in St. George, Utah.

In the evening, the new members of the Church assembled in Mr. Nickerson's house for confirmation. God bestowed his Spirit very freely and the Prophet gave much valuable instruction.

Two more persons came to the Prophet and requested baptism at the meeting the next day. It was attended to and a branch of the Church was organized. Freeman Nickerson was ordained as the presiding elder.

The evening of this day . . . the family were all seated around the wide, old-fashioned fireplace in the parlor listening to the Prophet's words and full of rejoicing.

"I would be so glad if someone who has been baptized could receive the gift of tongues as the ancient Saints did and speak to us," said Moses Nickerson.

"If one of you will rise up and open your mouth it shall be filled, and you shall speak in tongues," replied the Prophet.

Everyone then turned as by a common instinct to Lydia and said with one voice, "Sister Lydia, rise up."

And then the great glory of God was manifested to this weak but trusting girl. She was enveloped as with a flame, and unable longer to retain her seat, she rose and her mouth was filled with the praises of God and his glory. The spirit of tongues was upon her, and she was clothed in a shining light, so bright that all present saw it with great distinctness above the light of the fire and the candles.

Gates, *Lydia Knight's History*, pp. 20-22.

.

LYDIA   KNIGHT

"Here Is All I Have"

On reaching Kirtland, the family with whom Lydia had traveled set at once to make arrangements to settle down. Leaving his wife and Lydia at the hotel, Mr. Knight went out, soon returning with his brother Vincent Knight, who was a resident of Kirtland. On being introduced to Lydia, Vincent Knight said: "Sister, the Prophet is in bondage and has been brought into distress by the persecutions of the wicked, and if you have any means to give, it will be a benefit to him."

"Oh yes, sir," she replied, "here is all I have. I only wish it was more," emptying her purse, containing perhaps fifty dollars, in his hand as she spoke.

He looked at it and counted it and fervently exclaimed: "Thank God, this will release and set the Prophet free!"

The young girl was without means now, even to procure a meal or a night's lodging. Still that sweet spirit that rested upon her whispered "all will be well."

As evening drew on, Vincent Knight returned and brought the welcome news that Joseph was at liberty, and Lydia's joy to think that she had been the humble means of helping the Prophet was unbounded.

Gates, *Lydia Knight's History*, p. 25.

LYDIA KNIGHT

"Be Calm"

That evening [January 11, 1847] Newel [her husband] was buried. No lumber could be had, so Lydia had one of her wagon-boxes made into a rude coffin. The day was excessively cold, and some of the brethren had their fingers and feet frozen while digging the grave and performing the last offices of love for their honored captain and brother.

As the woman looked out upon the wilderness of snow and saw the men bearing away all that was left of her husband, it seemed that the flavor of life had fled and left only dregs, bitter, unavailing sorrow. But as she grew calmer she whispered with poor, pale lips, "God rules!"

Time was empty of incident or interest to Lydia until the 4th of February, when Brother Miller, who had been to Winter Quarters for provisions, returned and brought tidings of a revelation showing the order of the organization of the camp of the Saints, and also the joyful news that Brothers E. T. Benson and Erastus Snow were coming soon to Ponca to organize the Saints according to the pattern given in the revelation.

On the day of the organization, Lydia returned from the meeting and sat down in her home full of sad thoughts. How could she, who had never taken any care except that which falls to every woman's share, prepare herself and family to return to Winter Quarters and from thence take a journey a thousand miles into the Rocky Mountains? The burden weighed her very spirit down until she cried out in her pain, "Oh Newel, why hast thou left me!"

As she spoke, he stood by her side, with a lovely smile on his face, and said: "Be calm, let no sorrow overcome you. It was necessary that I should go. I was needed behind the veil. . . . You cannot fully comprehend it now; but the time will come when you shall know why I left you and our little ones. Therefore, dry up your tears. Be patient, I will go before you and protect you in your journeyings. And you and your little ones shall never perish for lack of food."

Gates, *Lydia Knight's History*, pp. 71-72.

"Stampedes"

It was here in this "buffalo country" that the famous stampedes of the animals were wont to take place. Without one second's warning, every ox and cow in the whole train would start to run, and go almost like a shot out of a gun. No matter how weary or how stupid they were, when one made the spring, the remainder of the horned stock were crazed with fear. On, on, they would go for miles, and seemed unable to stop until headed and brought back to camp.

One day while slowly plodding along beneath the burning, sultry sun, the start was made, and as every wagon was drawn by oxen or cows, away went cattle, wagons, and inmates; tin and brass pails, camp-kettles . . . jingling merrily behind and underneath the wagons where they were tied; children screaming, everything that was loose flying out as they bumped along. Over the untrodden prairie flew the maddened cattle, nearer and nearer to the river bank, which was here a precipice of twenty-five feet down to the water. Women, seeing their danger, sobbed out wild prayers for God to save; men ran and shouted to no avail; when suddenly over the plumy grass flew a horseman, spurring and screaming to his quivering, panting horse. Mothers clasped their frightened babes in their arms and prepare to face their watery grave. But the rider was up with the head team, and just as the head wagons were within ten feet of the deadly bank, he turned them aside and they were saved.

Lydia's wagon was near the lead, and she came within a few feet of the precipice. When she once more was safely traveling in the road, she and her children thanked God for his deliverance, praying that they might be so endangered no more. Her prayer was granted.

Gates, *Lydia Knight's History*, pp. 85-86.

"Lydia, Be Patient and Fear Not"

The little babe was a week old when a sudden severe rainstorm came up. It poured down into the cabin with much violence. Lydia told her daughter Sally to give her all the bedclothes they had, and these were put upon the bed and removed as they became soaked.

At last, finding the clothes were all wet completely through and that she was getting chilled sitting up in the wet, she said, "Sally, go to bed. It's no use doing any more unless some power beyond that which we possess is exercised; it is impossible for me to avoid catching cold. But we will trust in God; he has never failed to hear our prayers."

And so she drew her babe to her, and covered up as well as she could, and asked God to watch over them all through the night.

Her mind went back to the time when she had a noble companion, one who would never allow her to suffer any discomfort and who loved her as tenderly as man could woman. But now he was in the grave in a savage Indian country, and she was alone and in trouble.

As she thus mused, chilled with the cold rain and shivering, her agony at his loss became unbearable and she cried out, "Oh Newel, why could you not have stayed with and protected me through our journeyings?"

A voice plainly answered her from the darkness around her and said, "Lydia, be patient and fear not. I will still watch over you, and protect you in your present situation. You shall receive no harm. It was needful that I should go, and you will understand why in due time."

As the voice ceased, a pleasant warmth crept over her and seemed like the mild sunshine on a lovely spring afternoon.

Curling down in this comfortable atmosphere, she went immediately to sleep, and awoke in the morning all right, but wet to the skin.

Instead of receiving harm from this circumstance, she got up the next morning, although the child was but a week old, and went about her usual labors.

Gates, *Lydia Knight's History*, p. 73.

"Will We Eat This and Trust to Luck to Get the Tenth?"

When first moving into their little home [in Utah], Lydia had put all the cows but one upon the range. The following very remarkable instance is an example of what God will do for those who gladly keep his laws:

The one cow left at home stood out in the open air, staked a little way from the house. One morning in December Lydia awoke to find herself surrounded by a mountain of snow.

"Oh, the cow!" said Lydia, as she sprang from her bed. "Boys, something must be done."

Hurriedly dressing, she went to the door, and there stood the faithful beast, cold and shivering, and there was not a spear of feed to give her.

"Boys, take this blanket," said Lydia, taking a heavy, warm, homemade blanket from her bed, "and go down to Brother Drake, who lives in the Second Ward. I knew him in the Ponca camp, and something whispers to me that he will have some feed for the cow. Tell him I would like to get enough of some kind

60

of feed to last until this storm is over, and we can turn the poor thing out. This blanket is a good, almost new one, and should be worth part of a load."

The boys hastened down to Brother Drake's, and in a little while Lydia was pleased and surprised to see them returning in a wagon, which was well loaded with feed.

You may be sure Lydia thanked and blessed her kind friend; the boys went to work and made a pen of poles that they had hauled for wood, and they soon had "Bossie" in a warm place.

In the course of a day or two, Lydia was able to churn, getting just about a pound of butter. When it was all worked over, she said to the children who had watched the operation with much interest, "Now, children, what shall we do? Here is just about a pound of butter; we may not be able to get the tenth from the cow, and shall we pay this, the first pound for tithing, or will we eat this and trust to luck to get the tenth?"

"Pay this for tithing," answered all the children with one breath. "We can do without, mother, till you churn again."

So the butter was taken to the tithing office. That cow was a "stripper" (had no calf for two years), and furthermore, the cow never got a spear of feed but what Brother Drake had brought, it having lasted until the grass grew in the spring.

As Lydia has since told me, she has made it a firm rule to pay the first instead of the tenth of everything for tithing, commencing always with New Year's Day. "And," added she in relating this circumstance, "I have never been without butter in the house from that day to this."

Gates, *Lydia Knight's History*, pp. 93-94.

Biographical Sketch

LOUISE LAKE

POLIO! When she heard the dreaded diagnosis, Louise Lake didn't know how permanent her paralysis would be—she knew only that she had no feeling in her legs. What would happen to her? to her small daughter? How could she cope without mobility? Would she be unable to effectively function in her role as a mother and a homemaker?

Yes, she would! With great determination and even greater faith, she came back from the brink of death (the doctors had told her her case was hopeless) to become what one friend called "a miracle in modern Israel."

She learned to live each day, one day at a time, and to make the best of each situation. And along the way she found time to serve and inspire countless others throughout two continents.

Learning to cope with life in a wheelchair was more of an inconvenience than a handicap for Louise Lake, who received national recognition as the Outstanding Handicapped American of the Year—the first woman ever to be so honored. She conquered the problems of living alone and of working in the

nation's busiest city, New York. A group of international rehabilitation officials were astonished when she traveled alone
throughout South America, preaching what one world-famous
authority on rehabilitation for the physical handicapped called
the "gospel of rehabilitation." Her theme was "We are our
brother's keeper."

Elder Marion D. Hanks, Assistant to the Council of the
Twelve Apostles of The Church of Jesus Christ of Latter-day
Saints, who has known Louise for many years, sums up her life
story thus: "That one who has been confined to a wheelchair for
a quarter of a century and has suffered many serious afflictions
and much heartache should radiate so much of healing and
wholesomeness and motivate in others so much gratitude and renewed determination is unassailable witness that God can indeed 'consecrate our afflictions to our gain.' "

LOUISE LAKE

"The Great Window of Tomorrow"

Louise Lake tells of the struggle she had when stricken with polio:

An administrator of the hospital had located an iron lung not in use at a nearby army base, Jefferson Barracks. An ambulance with police escort was immediately sent to bring the iron lung to the hospital for my use. In the meantime, this young mother had been brought in for delivery of her baby. To the anxious doctors, her case seemed more hopeful than mine, for my condition had worsened and the doctors' hope for my life had fled. Thus, they placed the young mother in the emergency breather. Within a week she died. The last available machine had failed to save her. Polio also proved fatal to her infant.

Because I had held on so long without any assistance in breathing, the medical team decided to wait and see if I could get by without the lung. They felt that it was better for me to put up with the utter exhaustion, the pain and fever, the intervals with perspiration that were leaving me wet and dazed. Many times I muttered in a daze before lapsing again into a coma. One of my lungs collapsed, leaving the other to do all the work of breathing. Sometimes in the interminable night and daylight hours when I half revived, my surroundings seemed strange and I tried to focus my consciousness. Where was I? What was happening? By now my hands and arms were also paralyzed. I felt that I was burning up with fever, but I couldn't lift my arms and hands to wipe off my forehead. A craving grew in me to turn in bed, but I could not. I thirsted for a drink of water and a glass on the nearby table. But there was no muscle power in my hands and arms to reach out and take the water to quench my thirst. This tragic struggle seemed to be a never-ending nightmare.

One thing that always seemed to loom out whenever I looked in that direction was the black leatherbound book containing the latter-day scriptures that I had asked to take along. They were placed on a small table in the room. The letters in gold seemed to shine out—"The Book of Mormon," "Doctrine and Covenants," and "Pearl of Great Price." My face lighted up when I saw them. It was like looking through the great window of tomorrow. Somewhere in all of this was meaning. That sight is what made it easier for me to fight for life.

Another flash of consciousness came as I sought to use the call light button and could not. Finally I cried out for help. A nurse who was not afraid of isolation opened the screened-off area. As she came swiftly to the foot of my bed, I noted the white cap and white gauze mask on her shining black face. Feebly I mumbled some distress, and as if she had heard exact instructions, she took my left heel in one hand and placed her other hand under my left knee. Slowly and gently she raised the leg from the forced position it had been in for hours. There was some immediate relief. I hadn't known what to tell her to do for my comfort. Was she intuitive or knowledgeable? Anyway, she sensed my gratitude. She then quickly and silently passed to the opposite side of my bed, where she repeated this gesture of love with the other leg. I sighed warmly my appreciation to her. Then I said, "I feel so alone and in need of God's help. Will you pray with me?"

She at once stepped to the door and closed it tightly. Though she was risking her career, she came back to my side, dropped the isolation mask from her face, and took off her gloves. Taking my two helpless hands in her strong black hands, she lowered her head in reverence and said, "You'll have to pray—I can't."

Not the words, but only the feelings of my heart do I remember in that brief prayer when I sought for strength to endure. I thanked my Heavenly Father for the relief that had come in those moments of distress and for that nurse who had come like an angel to assist me. When I opened my eyes and looked up at her, tears were coursing down her face. Before she let go of my hands she looked into my face, also flooded with tears, and said, "I would give anything and have no fears if I knew God like that and could pray to him that way."

After that she slipped into my room many times to manipulate my legs and change their position. I never learned her name. Many times since I have wished that I could find her. Only God, that nurse, and I knew those cherished moments together that brought comfort and relief.

My oldest sister, Sarah Wild, had come to St. Louis when she heard by telephone that frightening report of my condition. I had been in a coma for several hours, and she was walking down the corridor in search of a snack shop or restaurant. One of the doctors who had observed her vigil outside my isolation door intercepted her and suggested firmly that she not leave. He said, "She will not be long. She is very near death."

Soon after he uttered those words, the branch president and three other men from the Church arrived; they wished to perform the sacred ordinance of administration, giving me a healing blessing and sealing it with prayer. Their request to enter my room was met with a blank refusal by the doctors. It was too late to pray for me, they were told. At that stage I was more dead than alive. Nevertheless, these men were firm in their desire and told the doctors that they had authority as ministers of the gospel of Jesus Christ, and were I fully conscious and rational, this would be my wish. With that they were told, "Okay. You can't help her, and you endanger yourselves with such exposure, but go ahead."

The elders were then led to a room where they scoured their hands like surgeons and put on gauze masks and long white medical gowns. Remarkably, as my door opened, I began to awaken suddenly. The incident is still fresh in my memory, and I trust it will be eternally. Fighting my way, as it were, out of a dense fog and deep sleep, I became aware that priesthood bearers had entered the room. I knew them and was fully conscious of why they had come. I couldn't speak, nor do I remember exactly what they said to me or to the Lord as they anointed me. But one thing I did know: as they placed their hands carefully on my head and invoked the blessings of our Heavenly Father, the whisperings of the Spirit of the Lord were filling my entire being with the message "You will live. You will live."

Louise Lake, *Each Day a Bonus* (Salt Lake City: Deseret Book Co., 1971), pp. 10-13.

LOUISE LAKE

"Yet Sings Knowing He Hath Wings"

Even the most severe moments were intertwined with a sense of peace.

One afternoon following the start of physical therapy treatment, I was resting in bed. As the sky darkened, there was a warm heavy spring rain. That day, defying the drench of the downpour, a robin came and stood for a moment or two outside my window ledge. The amazing thing was that he was singing his song while the water pelted on him. My eyes drank in this sight. It was like a gift, a new promise of life to me. The rain and darkened skies no longer made it a dreary day.

Only recently have I read Victor Hugo's lines:

> Be like the bird who, halting in his flight on a limb too slight
> Feels it give way beneath him,
> Yet sings knowing he hath wings.

68

The memory of that sight has remained a soul-filling lesson throughout the years.

In those hospital days I saw, as well as was the recipient of, considerate attention, patience, and forbearance. This place became my home. I like to think that nurses, doctors, and other patients felt the same way. . . .

One afternoon a pretty brunette nurse said she was planning marriage following her graduation. I asked about her wedding plans. In those days hats were a "must" in fashion, a kind of special frosting for any wedding. I at once took a leap in the light.

"Could I make your 'going-away' wedding hat?" I asked.

She hesitated. I knew she was wondering (1) what will it look like? and (2) where can you find the needed muscle power in your fingers and hands?

Quickly I assured her (I was also assuring myself) that in my pre-paralysis years I had attended millinery classes while living in Portland, Oregon. Techniques in making beautiful hats, as well as the styles in high fashion, were part of my stock in trade.

She breathed with relief and said, "I would love that."

Knowing her bridal colors, we combed the yellow pages of the telephone directory for a wholesale millinery outlet. Then I clumsily wrote out a list of materials and she set out to buy them.

Soon I was surrounded with needles, thread, buckram, trimmings, and all the other sewing sprawl. It was good that there were several weeks before the appointed day.

The adventure of hat making began. I struggled with the needle to make the stitches neat and strong. The weakness of my fingers and hands was more in focus. Though it was an exhausting task, the chapeau began to take form. I tired quickly and therefore rested frequently. None of us had realized what solid therapy this self-induced pressure would bring. Then one day it dawned on me that the muscles in my fingers and hands were definitely gaining strength and they could get stronger still!

It was President Heber J. Grant, that great master spirit in the building of the Church, who so beautifully taught this truth from Ralph Waldo Emerson: "That which we persist in doing comes easier for us to do; not that the nature of the thing itself as changed, but that our power to do is increased."

When the hat, which was by now a hospital conversation piece, was completed, there was wild enthusiasm among the nurses. A line on the right had formed, as each girl took her turn to have a favorite hat made. It took unlimited patience, but the working hours passed quickly. At times the room looked like the backroom of a millinery shop, and three large dresser drawers were full of hat supplies. The nurses and I kept it a secret that I was working for them. The doors would quickly open and close and a nurse would remove her white cap to try on her hat before the mirror. Whenever a supervisor or someone from the administration chanced to be around, the girl would scamper out of there like a chaff in the wind.

During the remainder of the time in the hospital I made fifteen hats. The girls looked *trés chic!* And the energy investment had paid off for me—not in dollars, for I naturally wouldn't accept money, but in the development of human resources. I was incredibly enriched. I hope many of those nurses have become happy grandmothers by now.

Lake, *Each Day a Bonus,* pp. 35-37.

LOUISE LAKE

"We Compare Ourselves With the Wrong People"

With little enthusiasm I wheeled toward the door of the hospital room, and as I passed by a bed near the doorway I stopped short. My eyes were drawn to the sight of a young woman, lying on her back, peering up as if she saw beyond the white ceiling. Her hair, prematurely gray, was pulled straight back from her face. Her soft blue eyes did not turn to look at me when I stopped. It was her striking countenance, deep in thought, that pulled me to a halt. I said, "Hello."

For the first time she turned her gaze to me. "Hello," she answered.

I studied her expression as I inquired of her health. I thought, What an unusually beautiful face! She looked worn, but there was also a look of patience. Written in that countenance were peace and serenity. You don't see that look on the faces of people in the streets. I was impressed. I was in the presence of one who had gone that mile alone. And she had come through. How green I was. It was less than three years that I had known my handicap. There was not the slightest tension between us. It was close to the bone and touched a few nerves within me— more so when I learned that her name was Louise Johnson, the same as my maiden name.

She asked about my shiny new wheelchair. I inquired as to her knowledge of chairs. Did she know about chairs? "Yes," she said. "I used to be in one." I must have looked puzzled. Out from under the white sheets she brought her hands, folded together, and carefully placed them on top of the bed covers. The fingers of each hand, gnarled and twisted, looked as though they had been laced together. They were so distorted that it was a shock to me.

"You see," she continued, "when my hands became so bent with arthritis, I could no longer wheel a chair. Before that only my feet and legs were involved."

I quietly gasped, "How long has that been?"

She replied, "Well, I have been confined here to the bed for eleven years."

I was stunned. I had really been off balance. I changed my despondent thinking fast. Instead, with all my heart, I was silently praying for her. Over and over again I was silently saying, "God bless her and help her!" Before going there I had been to busy looking for the easy—and pleasing to me—way of life.

When I returned home, my own confusions had greatly lessened. I thought, "This has been a wonderful night. I must remember it through the years." So I have done. Far too often we compare ourselves with the wrong people—those who seem to possess everything. How good it is for us to compare ourselves with the right people. We will quickly count that which we have and build our houses of happiness.

Lake, *Each Day a Bonus*, pp, 74-75.

LOUISE LAKE

"A Special Spiritual Thanksgiving"

There was a knock on my back door. I opened the door to see Brother [Matthew] Cowley standing there with a large frozen turkey in his arms. With a twinkle in his eye he said, "Here, take this. We received two turkeys." I replied, "Oh, I shouldn't take that, Brother Cowley. You folks can cook it later." He said, "Don't you think we should prepare ourselves to live the United Order? Let folks do things for you and don't deprive them of blessings from God."

So I took the turkey with much appreciation. It was a little less than a week before Thanksgiving day. Having this plump holiday bird gave me the bright idea of giving a Thanksgiving dinner party. The Beehive House across the street, I thought, would probably have only two or three girls there during that holiday weekend. The other girls would be returning to their own homes. There were two gracious, lovable matrons who gave that home its tone and atmosphere and who directed life there.

They were Florence Smith and Verna Jensen. They told me that their Thanksgiving dinner was to be held the Sunday preceding Thanksgiving, so the girls could scamper in their different directions for the big turkey day.

Now I hadn't planned on this, but I felt as if a large bell were beating in my head, encouraging me. Suddenly I forgot my own troubles; I would slip over all concern and conversation about the broken leg. Changing the subject was better.

I learned that eight girls would be remaining in the Beehive House, so I invited them to my dinner.

For two days I cooked up a storm, wheeling in circles around the kitchen and doubling (or more!) traditional recipes. I could hardly close the refrigerator door, for it held a careful arrangement of everything good to eat. Then I gathered up all of my table finery.

Thanksgiving morning came. To be sure that no one would be alone and perhaps lonely, I asked a special prayer that morning. I asked Heavenly Father to direct any girl who was alone and without promise of dinner to come to my door. About ten-thirty the doorbell rang. When I answered, there stood a girl from our MIA group. She had dropped by to wish me a happy Thanksgiving. "Where are you going to dinner?" I asked. When she replied that she didn't have an invitation for dinner, I insisted that she must return. "You're coming here. Be here by two-thirty!"

About two-thirty the guests began arriving. I didn't know those nine girls well, but that didn't matter. They were all away from home, and they very likely would have been lonely.

It certainly didn't take long for everyone to feel at home. What a vast store of exhilaration was mine as we bustled about, placing dishes of hot delicious food on the table. The luscious brown turkey was surrounded by all of the customary festive trimmings, and there was a choice of three rich and flavorful desserts.

I still see a picture of eleven gracious and beautiful girls, my daughter included, encircled in warmth and love around the well-spread banquet table. I thought of them as rare jewels sharing a special spiritual Thanksgiving in the soft glow of the candlelight.

Lake, *Each Day a Bonus*, pp. 77-78.

LOUISE LAKE

"They Placed Their Hands on Jane's Head"

Jane [Louise's daughter], who was then about fifteen years old, became ill and was feeling too miserable to get out of bed. After a couple of days of the illness, the doorbell rang with a familiar ring. When I opened the door, Matthew Cowley stood there. He said, "I haven't seen you folks lately. How are you?"

"Well," said I, "Jane is sick and I have no idea why. Would you like to step inside and see her?" He came in and put his head around the doorway of the bedroom to speak to her. After his cheerful greeting she asked, "Brother Cowley, would you please give me a blessing?"

"You bet," came the answer. After pausing a few seconds and moving back down the hallway to the front door, he said, "I will be back in a little while."

A short time later the doorbell rang again. Upon opening the door I saw two men—Elder Cowley and a Polynesian friend by his side. He had often told us of the simple but powerful faith of those great Pacific Island folks. He had gone to find Elder Wi Peri Amaru to assist in giving the blessing my teenager had requested. I took them into the bedroom.

There were twin beds in the room. Jane was in the bed nearest the wall, and it was therefore necessary for them to cross over the room to her. I sat silently a little way inside of the door. After introducing his fine-looking companion, Elder Cowley dropped to his knees by the bedside. His friend followed. They placed their hands on Jane's head, and Brother Cowley's friend gave a wonderful spiritual blessing.

The tears coursed down my face at that sight and the witness that I sat near the presence of angels. The man spoke fluently in the Maori tongue as he uttered the blessing. It was indeed a spiritual experience to behold this choice apostle of the Lord and his worthy friend as they knelt and petitioned our Heavenly Father in Jane's behalf in our humble home.

I thought, No wonder Brother Cowley says "No man is greater than when he is on his knees praying!"

Immediately following the blessing, they departed. As he was about to close the door, Brother Cowley (knowing I did not understand the Maori language) said, "Someday I will tell you something about that blessing."

The next day the doctor told me that Jane must go to the hospital because she had pneumonia. She made a speedy recovery there.

After she returned home and was well, one day Brother Cowley said, "Now that's what was told her that day in the blessing—that she would be sicker and it was necessary for her to go to the hospital. But she was also blessed with a quick recovery. I didn't tell you at that time because I didn't want you to worry about it."

Lake, *Each Day a Bonus*, pp. 86-87.

Biographical Sketch

ETTIE LEE

Ettie Lee was born in Luna Valley, New Mexico Territory, on November 2, 1885, the second daughter and fourth child of John David Lee and Evaline Dorinda Clark.

After her graduation from the Gila Academy in Thatcher, Arizona, she began her illustrious teaching career at age seventeen, in the year 1903. After three years she attended the Northern Arizona Normal School. She then went to southern California, taught in night school, and furthered her education at the University of Southern California.

Ettie Lee had a great love for the underprivileged and wayward, and by using her extraordinary energy and ability in wise real estate investments she became well-to-do financially, which permitted her to finance and build homes for troubled boys.

On one occasion Ettie Lee was honored as the woman who had done most for youth in the Los Angeles area. One of the speakers eulogized her as follows: "She may well be the nation's foremost enemy of delinquency because of the pattern she has set."[1]

---

[1]Ora Pate Stewart, *Tender Apples* (Salt Lake City: Deseret Book Co., 1965), p. 330.

ETTIE LEE

"He Has Listed You as Next of Kin"

Ettie was arranging the things on her desk, preparing for class, when suddenly Robert, a handsome lad of fifteen, ran past her, around the desk, and into her arms, sobbing hopelessly.

"What is it, Robert?" Ettie consoled.

The boy looked helplessly around the room, under the desk, into the corridor. "You'll have to hide me, Miss Lee. The cops! They'll be here any minute."

Ettie tightened her arms around his trembling body.

"What is the trouble, son? Why are they after you?"

The boy placed a pistol on her desk, almost threw it.

"It isn't loaded, Miss Lee. Honest, I wouldn't pull a *loaded* gun. The clip is empty. I didn't do anything *wrong*. Ya gotta believe me, Miss Lee. Tell 'em I didn't do anything wrong."

Ettie guided him to her chair. "Sit down here, Robert, and let's start at the first. Where did you get the gun, and what did you need it for?"

"It's my dad's. He brought it home from the war. He took it off a German soldier. I wasn't going to shoot anybody. I know better than to kill people. Cam Smith wanted to buy it and I was

78

bringing it to school to show him. He was gonna give me three dollars for it."

"Cam Smith has left school; he's nineteen."

"I know, Miss Lee, but he was gonna meet me here with the money. But when I turned into 32nd Street, Cam was there and he pulled me into that little shack next to the candy store and told me he had a plan. I was to wait in the shack until the man came to open the candy store, and then I was to step out and say, 'Stick 'em up.' When the man gave me his money, I was to keep three dollars of it and give the rest to Cam. I said I didn't want to do it, and Cam said, 'Sure you do; how else do you expect me to git you the three dollars?' I told him I didn't want to, and he called me chicken."

"Oh, Robert, that is such an old, old trap."

"I guess it is. We waited until the man came and unlocked the candy store—and guess who were his first customers? Two men from the firehouse around the corner. I waited until they'd gone, and then I did like Cam told me. But just as I was getting ready to say it, I noticed Cam running down the street as fast as he could go, and one of the firemen was chasing him. The other one came running back into the store and asked to use the phone. He said, 'That worthless Smith kid was hanging around that shack . . . he's up to something.' And he called the cops, and the storekeeper said, 'You was with him, wasn't you?' and I said 'No'; and he said, 'Then what are you standin' there holdin' that gun for?' and he reached under the counter, and I got out of there. But I left my books, and they know where to come to get me. They'll be here any minute."

Ettie figured her time with him was short. She wanted to make the most of it. There might never be another chance.

"Robert, I'll have to talk fast; but *please remember*. Please remember everything I am going to say: It was all wrong. It was wrong for your father to take the gun off a German soldier; but it was wartime, and we'll have to excuse him. It was wrong for you to attempt to sell it when it was not yours. What were you planning to tell your father when he missed it? Never mind, it would surely have been an untruth. But the biggest danger of all was to your own life. The storekeeper could not possibly be expected to know that your gun was not loaded, and he could have shot you down—and he would have gone free—self-defense, guarding his own life and property. By the time the police discovered that your gun was not loaded you would be lying in the morgue, and your parents would have lost a fine son; would have lost him under a cloud of disappointment and anguish, in a sorrow that no parents deserve.

"Robert, your whole life is before you. You have a splendid future if you will establish your values early—get it straight what is right and what is wrong—set some good goals and work toward them. Stay away from those who try to lead you into temptation.

"And now, Robert, I think it will go easier for you if we go to the front office and wait for the officers, rather than compel them to search every room. I think we had best leave the gun here; you can put it in my drawer and we will lock it up. If they need it they can come here for it. If they saw you with it in your hand they just might think you were dangerous, and there could be more trouble. The children will be coming in; let us go quickly.

"And Robert, remember that there are those who care, very, very much."

Ettie was proud as Robert walked ahead of her toward the officers.

"I believe I am the boy you are looking for," he said with a courage that she had not entirely expected. "The gun is in the drawer. It is not loaded."

When they left, it was Ettie who was crying. She wondered how it would go with the boy. Other boys had disappeared from the classroom from time to time—to turn up after ninety days, or six months, or a year, with a reform school record and a fresh set of bad habits. One or two had graduated to prison.

When Ettie was called to the office an hour later, she approached the phone with great anxiety.

"Miss Lee? Would you be willing to look after this young man for a probation of about a year? He has listed you as next of kin. He says he would like to go to school and learn to amount to something."

Who says prayers don't get through?

———————

Stewart, *Tender Apples*, pp. 237-41.

———————

"To My Friend, Ettie Lee"

A book could be written about the experiences of Ettie Lee as an apartment house owner. Some of the episodes are humorous, some pathetic, some are exciting, and all are interesting. But here is one story that does not lend itself to generality. It must be told all by itself.

Ettie was hunting for a woman of special ability to manage a sixty-unit apartment house. Like the old woman who lived in a shoe, the woman who manages sixty units has her hands full. She must be a woman of patience and understanding. Besides all the human virtues, she must possess an unfailing business ability, because a sixty-unit apartment is a big business, and it had better not fail. She must be something of an appraiser of human character. And she must be just the right blend of the mother-confessor and the aloof, detached, impersonal friend. And withal, she must be a top saleswoman.

The depression was on. Any number of women wanted work. But Ettie realized, knew from experience, that was a special order. She inquired around from trusted people of judgment.

"Yes," one of her janitors informed her, "I know of such a woman—a widow, about forty-five, trying to put her son through college. Pleasant and capable. She's honest through and through. A woman you'll like."

That was good enough for Ettie Lee. She went to the address.

From the very first Ettie knew that Alicia Bringhurst was the right woman. She arranged for Mrs. Bringhurst to have the front apartment, a double, with full bedroom and the roll-away so that her son could have a home while attending USC. It was within walking distance, and the woman and her son were grateful for that.

Time went on. The young man graduated from USC, got a job, married a pretty bride, and moved to an apartment of his own. The depression lifted somewhat, and jobs were easier to find. For ten years Ettie did not have to worry about her sixty-unit house. The rents came in; tenants were satisfied; management was happy; bookkeeping was accurate. All was well.

And then one morning Ettie's phone rang. Alicia Bringhurst would be leaving now. Her son had moved his wife and three children into a comfortable house in Brentwood, and Alicia would go to live with them. Ettie had it on her tongue's end to say that those arrangements never work out; but she also had the good taste to allow others to live their own lives. She expressed her honest appreciation for Mrs. Bringhurst's faithful service and her sorrow that she would be losing her most capable manager, and offered her most heartfelt best wishes for Alicia's happiness in her new home.

Actually, Ettie was bewildered. She had hoped that Mrs. Bringhurst would stay on a least another ten years. Wages were good, conditions pleasant. Ettie could not figure out why she should leave so abruptly.

Brentwood was a long-distance call, and Ettie more or less lost track. But one day, after about six months, Bob Bringhurst called her about a character reference for a new job, and Ettie had a chance to ask him about his mother.

"Why, didn't you know?" the young man said, surprised. "Mother is now totally blind."

"She is *what?*" Surely she had not heard it right.

"It has been coming on for more than a year. It is an outgrowth of her diabetic condition."

"Her what?"

"Yes, she was an advanced diabetic before the blindness set in. I guess you didn't know, then, that that was why she left you."

"Is she with you? May I talk with her?"

"No, Aunt Ettie, we had to put her in a rest home. Janice just couldn't stand the strain of having her around. She felt so tied down all the time. Janice said she had to save her strength for the children. After all, a mother always feels that her children come first. As Janice says, no house is big enough for three generations. She just couldn't take it any longer, having a blind person around. So I took Mother to Rest Haven." (That is not its proper name.)

Ettie got the address and hurried out to see Alicia.

It was heartbreaking. There were a dozen or so women at the shabby "home." Some were obviously mental cases, needing much more care than the place provided. . . .

She found Alicia alone on a sagging back porch. Her hair was almost white, and she looked twenty pounds thinner and a good ten years older than she had been six months before. Ettie put her arms around her and kissed her. Alicia cried. . . .

How could anyone leave a woman who was so fine and capable, so sensitive, who had done so much for humanity, in a place like this!

"Oh, it is not so bad," Alicia said, forcing a smile. "My blind pension pays for it all. I will never be a burden to my son."

"I am sure you will not!" Ettie's temper was uncommonly roused. No manager of hers was going to end up in a sty such as this! "Get your things. We're leaving this minute!"

"I have no place to go, Ettie. You forget, I am totally blind."

"We'll find a place. In the meantime you are coming home with me." . . .

As soon as there was a vacancy in one of her apartment houses Ettie took Alicia to her new home.

"But Ettie, there is not enough in my blind pension to afford such a lovely, convenient place," the woman protested.

"But, my dear, if you knew how badly I need your help in this apartment building, you would help me out, I know. The manager here is a young woman with practically no experience. She will need advice on so many things. I need you here to give her your wisdom and experience. I want her to feel free to call on you whenever she has a problem."

Ettie spent one whole day walking with her, counting the steps to the kitchen, the refrigerator, the stove, the cupboards, and the table; getting her direction to the bathroom—placing her hand on the new toothbrush; locating the telephone, memorizing important numbers; arranging her medications where they could be found with safety.

"Oh, Ettie," Alicia wept, "I will never complain again about anything as long as I live. Can you realize the luxury of having a bathroom all to yourself!"

Ettie brought a blind friend of many years to visit Alicia. She was able to show her many shortcuts and conveniences. She contacted the Society of the Blind and they sent tutors to teach her Braille, brought her books and records, a record player, and taught her useful skills.

The blind pension paid for the food and clothing she required, and with the apartment free, Alicia was set up in comfort and security for the rest of her life. And oh, was she pleased! She learned to do for herself with remarkable mastery, and her apartment was always spotless.

Ettie called on her often; and Alicia always offered her some little dainty, a bowl of strawberries, a piece of warm gingerbread, a hot biscuit and marmalade—things made especially for a guest. . . .

It had been eight years since Alicia had come to her new apartment home. Then one day she phoned Ettie and asked her if she would come and go with her to the doctor's office. She was feeling wonderful, she said; but this was the day she was supposed to go for her regular check-up.

There was no answer to Ettie's knock, but the door was ajar. She opened it and called to Alicia. She went into the kitchen. There on the table was a lovely cake, a golden angel food, decorated most artistically, bearing the words "To My Friend, Ettie Lee."

It was her last message. On the floor beyond the table, with the decorating tube still in her hand, lay the lifeless remains of Alicia Bringhurst. Her grateful heart had beat its last in doing this beautiful deed for her friend.

Stewart, *Tender Apples*, pp. 267-74.

RACHEL LEE*

"Tightly Bound to the Wheel"

Though the days were often dull, there were other times when the excitement was almost more than these prairie women needed, as Rachel Lee found out near the end of her journey. As she walked beside her wagon, delighting in the wind that cooled her a little as she trudged along, an unexpected gust whipped her skirts into the wagon wheel. Historical writer Juanita Brooks wrote that before Rachel knew it, her skirts were being "wrapped around and around the hub. She screamed for help as she tried to extricate them, but in an instant they were drawn so tight that she could only grasp two spokes in her hands, her feet between two others, and make a complete revolution with the wheel."

The wagon was finally stopped, and Rachel found herself almost right side up but still tightly bound to the wheel. Everyone gathered around, trying to decide how to get her loose. There was no question of cutting her clothing, as that would mean one less item for wear that she needed badly.

*Rachel Woolsey Lee was born August 5, 1825. She married John Doyle Lee in 1845, and they had eight children. She died in 1912 in Lebanon, Arizona.

It was decided they would unhook her skirt and unbutton the petticoat, and by carefully slitting the placket, she could be pulled free. Her shoes were unlaced. Then, as one woman held a blanket to protect her from curious eyes, she was plucked from skirt, petticoats, and shoes "clean as though they were skinning the legs of a chicken." Later the clothing was easily removed from the wheel, and in the privacy of her wagon, Rachel shook them free of wrinkles and put them on again. As she took up her walk again, she kept a wary distance from the wheels.

Kenneth and Audrey Ann Godfrey, "The Pioneer Woman," *Improvement Era,* May 1969, p. 34.

Biographical Sketch

LARUE C. LONGDEN

LaRue C. Longden is the wife of the late Elder John Longden, Assistant to the Council of the Twelve of The Church of Jesus Christ of Latter-day Saints. For nearly fourteen years she served as counselor in the general presidency of the Young Women's Mutual Improvement Association. During this time she directed the dance, drama, music, speech, sports, athletics, and camping programs of the YWMIA. Her work brought her in close contact with youth and their leaders, and she developed a keen sense of their needs and how to inspire them to live close to the Lord.

A talented musician, Sister Longden also is active in literary and dramatic circles. However, she says she loves most her career as a wife and mother. She and Elder Longden are the parents of two daughters, Mrs. Grant A. (Carolyn) Hickman and Mrs. Loren C. (Frances Sharon) Dunn (Loren C. Dunn is a member of the First Council of the Seventy), and several grandchildren.

Sister Longden has traveled throughout the world for the YWMIA and also accompanied her husband on many of his assignments. Her life has been one of service and love—to her husband, her children, and the Church.

LARUE C. LONGDEN

"A Beautiful Pattern for Living"

Long years ago when I was in my teens (yes, I remember those days very well!) I wanted to make myself a dress. I was very impetuous and decided to start it right away—immediately—without a pattern or any other guide. My mother said she was sure if I would wait and use a pattern, the results would be much more satisfactory. I thought I knew what I was doing, so I went ahead and cut the dress, whipped it up on the machine, then proceeded to try it on. Guess what? It was too short and too wide—the stripes didn't match down the back and at least a dozen other things were wrong with it. It did make a beautiful duster for the furniture. It seemed that piece of material would never wear out. It was always there to remind me of my folly. My darling mom said, "You'd have been smart to use a pattern, wouldn't you?"

That silly little incident has stayed with me all my life. I have come to know it is smart to have a pattern for living, if we would not waste our lives. It is smart to be a Latter-day Saint! Latter-day Saints have a beautiful pattern for living.

LaRue C. Longden, *It's Smart to Be a Latter-day Saint* (Salt Lake City: Deseret Book Co., 1967), pp. 1-2.

"This Man Knows the Shepherd"

The story is told of a great actor who, at the end of several curtain calls, repeated the 23rd Psalm for his audience. As he finished the applause was deafening. The audience stood and shouted, "More, more!" The actor had seen a man in the service of God near the front of the theater, and quieting the audience, he called the good man to the stage and asked him to repeat the 23rd Psalm. As the man finished, there was a dead silence, and a feeling of sweet spirituality seemed to permeate the theater. It was too sacred to applaud. The actor stepped forward and, with his arm around the man, said, "I know the words of the 23rd Psalm. This man knows the Shepherd."

What a thrilling experience is in store for all young people who will come to know the Shepherd because daily, hourly, every minute of their lives they listen to the promptings of the still, small voice, which is his gift to them to keep them safe, secure, and happy for eternity!

Longden, *It's Smart to Be a Latter-day Saint*, pp. 15-16.

"A Royal Inheritance"

Some time ago, a lovely young couple called at our home with some questions that needed answering—would I take time to help them? They looked so solemn and serious I thought that I was going to need the wisdom of Solomon to help them. I was rather relieved when they asked, "What does it mean to be 'worthy' to go to the temple?"

So we sat down and spent a pleasant evening exchanging confidences. They helped me and I hope I helped them. They were such a happy, dear couple that my heart swelled with pride to think, There are several hundred thousand just like them all over the world—noble Latter-day Saint youth!

This couple were soon to be married in the Salt Lake Temple. I told them that there are many things that enter into being a "worthy" Latter-day Saint. First of all, we must remember that the church to which we belong is of Jesus Christ. We are his Latter-day Saints. He is our elder brother. He set down some worthwhile and beautiful standards by which we must live. For instance, a worthy Latter-day Saint lives a clean life, obeys the Word of Wisdom, honors the priesthood, pays tithing, attends priesthood, sacrament, and all other Church meetings, loves his neighbor as himself, and loves his Father in heaven.

I asked them to tell me why they wanted to be married in the temple. As they sat together on the couch holding hands, their eyes lighted up and they said almost in unison, "Because we love each other and we want to be together always." I found, though, that there were several things they did not quite understand. They thought we were "a little too strict" in our requirements to enter the temple. This gave me the opportunity to tell one of my favorite stories. It is the true story of Queen Elizabeth.

The lovely Princess Elizabeth was carefully reared and trained to become Queen of England. She was taught that there are rules and regulations by which she must live and which she must honor if she would be a queen. She was taught what she must do when she came into her inheritance. She must never do anything that would bring disgrace to England.

Her courtship was guarded. Her marriage must be to one who could share her royalty. The children from that marriage . . . , because of their parents, now have a royal heritage that will continue if they comply with the rules that have been established. If they do not choose to do so, they cannot be admitted to the family circle or come into their royal heritage—they will have sold their birthright for a mess of pottage.

We saw a beautiful color motion picture made at the time Elizabeth ascended to her throne. I was thrilled and touched by the simplicity and modesty of her attire; in fact, with the naturalness of her everyday life. She was just a lovely young girl who had lived true to her beliefs, who had been trained for queenhood. At the time she entered the holy of holies we were not permitted to see or to hear what went on, but we were told that she was anointed to be Queen of England. When she came from this ceremony, she then was allowed to wear the royal robes of a queen.

My dear young couple, doesn't it make you tingle to realize how like these are the royal plans made for Latter-day Saint youth? You are taught what your duties are if you would come into royal inheritance. Boys and girls alike must live above reproach, being "honest, true, chaste, benevolent," honoring the priesthood and obeying the teachings of the gospel. Your courtships are guarded. If you would claim your royal inheritance, your marriage must be to one who shares your worthiness and your beliefs.

What is your royal inheritance? You were valiant in the councils in heaven, else you would not be here today. And you may, if you live worthily, be a king and a queen in the kingdom of God—forever. Yes, forever! You will have each other and your children and their children for all eternity! Does it seem that these regulations are too strict for such a royal reward? Is it too much to ask that you honor and respect your earthly bodies, which house the spirit children of our Father in heaven? Or is it too much to ask that you keep those bodies clean and pure, that some day you may go into partnership with our Father in bringing others of his spirit children to earth?

To be an eternal king and queen—does it seem too strict to ask you to adhere to the Word of Wisdom so you may reap the promises made by our Father that you may "have hidden treasures of knowledge," that you may "run and not be weary, and walk and not faint," that the "destroying angel may pass you by and not slay you"?

To be worthy to wear the robes of royalty in God's kingdom —do you think our modest dress standards are "a little too strict" for that? Let's think about it. What happens when young people are immodest in dress? Unkind, sometimes vulgar remarks are made about them. Too many times immodesty is the forerunner of unchastity. Unchastity brings unhappines, sorrow, and bitterness to all concerned. Is it too much to ask that Latter-day Saint boys and girls be modest—modest in speech, refraining from participating in unclean jokes and from taking the name of our Lord in vain; modest in actions or modest in dress? The royal robes of the priesthood are modest. If we would wear them, we must be modest too.

As the young couple left our home that evening, they had decided that we weren't too strict after all. They knew more than ever that they wanted to go to the temple and be married, that they too might look forward to being a king and queen in the hereafter and reign in their own kingdom. They knew they had been rewarded for being valiant in their very existence by being given healthy bodies and being allowed to come to this mortal earth to "prove themselves worthy." They truly wanted to return home to their Heavenly Father and Mother.

Longden, *It's Smart to Be a Latter-day Saint*, pp. 18-22.

LARUE C. LONGDEN

"Happy Home Hours"

There is a nostalgic peace that comes over many of us who have reached the half century mark when we recall our younger days. We are the fortunate ones who have tasted of unhurried existence. We remember happy evenings around the dining room table or in the "parlor" when mother sewed and father read from the evening paper, the scriptures, or the classics. Some of us recall being asked to "speak a piece" or to sing, play the piano, or in some way perform for loving, proud, doting parents who assured us that we were perfectly wonderful! There were discussions on current events, questions answered about "what we believe"; problems discussed and, if possible, cleared up; then, maybe a dish of ice cream—which, in those days, was a real treat; then the sweet togetherness of family prayer before going to bed. All this not on just one particular appointed night, but on many, many nights! Happy, happy memories! Such a feeling of surety that we would be "kept safe and sound throughout the night—that we would rise on the morrow healthy and strong, with a desire in our hearts to serve him."

If all children could be given a taste of this sort of happy living, there surely wouldn't be too much need for corrective institutions or even divorce courts. We no longer teach our children the old poems like "The Children's Hour," by Longfellow. It must be forty years ago when I learned:

Between the dark and the daylight,
When the night is beginning to lower,
Comes a pause in the day's occupations
That is known as the Children's Hour.

I still remember the warm feeling I had as I repeated all the verses of this lovely poem and I thought to myself, we are like that family. I could not have put it into words then, but I

95

realize today that in my youthful mind I knew that we, too, in our home had precious hours together; that there was a sweet love and precious spirituality pervading those hours spent together as a family.

The knowledge of man has given us many refinements in our homes. It has made mother's work much easier than it was in what our youngsters are pleased to call "the olden days." But that very knowledge of man has helped to push the wisdom and spirit of our Father in heaven into a too obscure background in many homes. Most families have too many outside interests.

I am not one who looks back and wishes we could return to the good old days—those good old days of washboards, coal stoves, horses and buggies. Not I! However, I would recapture for my beloved teenagers the quiet peace of evenings. . . .

There must be a happy medium. There is! It is up to Latter-day Saint parents to invite and then keep the sweet spirit of our Father in heaven in our homes by letting our children know that we love them, that they are very important to us, and their happiness, our main concern. Happy home hours can do much to knit families together.

Longden, *It's Smart to Be a Latter-day Saint,* pp. 28-30.

LARUE C. LONGDEN

"Happy Memories"

A young girl before leaving home to attend college asked her parents if they might have a family powwow, as she called it. She said, "Mom and dad, I want to thank you for trusting me enough to let me go away to college. I know at times we haven't quite agreed on some things, and I have probably caused you some worry. I want you to know that I am going to live as a Latter-day Saint girl should live."

Her father replied, "That is quite a big statement, dear; to live as a Latter-day Saint should live in this day and age takes real fortitude."

This little girl has been in college two years now and in talking with her she admitted that it hadn't been easy, even among her own Latter-day Saint friends. "But," she said, "I want to build happy memories and how else can I do this unless I build my life of virtuous, lovely, good materials?"

We wish you might all know this girl because she is so much fun, loves life with such a zest and is so lovely to look at . . . spiritually beautiful.

Longden, *It's Smart to Be a Latter-day Saint,* p. 39.

LARUE C. LONGDEN

"God Has Invited You"

While very young (and I thought I knew so much) I recall telling a dear Sunday School teacher that I was not going to sacrament meeting any more because it was so boring and dry. In great disgust Sister Hunter looked at me and said, "Don't you ever let me hear you say that again! God has invited you to that meeting to partake the emblems of Jesus Christ's suffering and of his gift to you. You are very privileged to be invited. If you take the right spirit with you to meeting, you will always bring something good away with you."

Dear Sister Hunter! That was half a century ago and I never have forgotten it. What's more, I've proven she was right. It isn't always easy to attend church, but if we are to learn more about what we believe and how we fit into the scheme of things in this old world, sacrament meeting is one good place—the only place—to be found at church time on Sunday. There we truly commune with the spirit of Heavenly Father and Jesus Christ. There we are spurred on in our search for the truth.

Longden, *It's Smart to Be a Latter-day Saint,* p. 106.

Biographical Sketch

ELIZABETH CLARIDGE McCUNE

Elizabeth Ann Claridge McCune was born February 19, 1852, at Leighton-Buzzard, Bedfordshire, England, a daughter of Samuel and Charlotte Joy Claridge. Her parents immigrated to Utah in 1853.

She was married to Alfred William McCune in 1872; he became a prominent and successful businessman. They were the parents of nine children.

In 1905 Sister McCune was appointed as a trustee of the Utah Agricultural College in Logan, Utah (now Utah State University). She served for ten years, and for two of those years she was vice-president of the board. A patron of the National Council of Women of the United States and of the International Council, she attended the International Congress of Women in London in 1899.

Elizabeth Claridge McCune was called to serve as a counselor in the general presidency of the Young Ladies' Mutual Improvement Association in 1888 and later served as a member of the general board of that organization. She was also a temple ordinance worker for twenty years. In 1911 she was called by President Joseph F. Smith to be a member of the general board of the Relief Society.

The McCunes were patrons of art and lovers of beauty. In 1920 they gave their beautiful mansion to the Church to be used as the Church leaders would choose. Most fittingly it was used for the Latter-day Saint School of Music.

The following tribute was given to Sister McCune following her death by five of her friends: "She loved much, she forgave more; she gave generously and withheld wisely. She was loved by many, admired and respected by all."

Elizabeth Ann Claridge McCune died August 1, 1924.

———

ELIZABETH CLARIDGE McCUNE

"I Know That My Father Will Go"

No place on earth seemed so precious to me at fifteen years of age as dear old Nephi [Utah]. How eagerly we looked forward to the periodical visits of President Brigham Young and his company! Everything was done that could be thought of for their comfort and entertainment. And with all it was a labor of love. One of these visits I shall never forget.

We went out with our Sabbath Schools and all the other organizations, with bands of music and flags and banners and flowers, to meet and greet our beloved leader and his company. On this occasion the people were lined up on each side of the street waiting for the carriages to pass. Among them were twenty-five young ladies dressed in white, who had strewn evergreens and wild flowers along the path. Brother Brigham, Brothers Kimball and Wells,[1] with the entire company, got out of their carriages and walked over the flowery road. When Brother Kimball passed me he said to the group of girls around me, "You five girls right here will live to be mothers in Israel."

---

[1] The First Presidency of the Church—Brigham Young, Heber C. Kimball, and Daniel H. Wells.

The company having been taken to our home, the dinner was served. How we girls flew around to make everything nice for the stylish city folks! As soon as they were seated at dinner, we slipped upstairs and tried on all the ladies' hats. That was a real treat. I venture to say that could the ladies have seen us next Sunday they would have been struck with the similarity of styles in Nephi and Salt Lake City millinery.

We all attended the afternoon meeting, the girls in white having reserved seats in front. The sermons were grand, and we were happy until President Young said that he had a few names to read of men who were to be called and voted in as missionaries to go and settle up the "Muddy." This almost stilled the beating of the hearts of all present. Many of our friends had been called to go to settle the Dixie country, but the "Muddy," so many miles farther south and so much worse! Oh! Oh! I did not hear another name except Samuel Claridge. Then how I sobbed and cried, regardless of the fact that the tears were spoiling the new white dress. The father of the girl who sat next to me was also called. Said my companion, "Why, what are you crying about? It doesn't make me cry. I know my father won't go." "Well, there is the difference," said I; "I know that my father will go and that nothing could prevent him, and I should not own him as a father if he would not go when he is called." Then I broke down sobbing again.

Everything occurred to prevent my father from getting off. Just as he was nearly ready to start, one of his horses got poisoned. He had to buy another horse. A week later one of his big mules was found choked to death in his barn. Some of our friends said, "Brother Claridge, this shows you are not to go." My father answered, "It shows me that the adversary is trying to prevent me from going, but I shall go if I walk!"

Susan Young Gates, *Memorial to Elizabeth Claridge McCune* (Salt Lake City, 1924), pp. 17-18.

"Spreading Each Piece With Molasses"

About three years after I was married I took my baby and traveled from Nephi to Long Valley, on a visit to my parents. I started with Brother Stewart and his daughter Ella, and wrote for my father to meet me at the place called Ham's Ranch. When we got there my father had not arrived. Thinking he would soon come, I stayed, and Brother Stewart went on to Kanab. The next morning he did not come, and then I knew that he had missed the letter. Remembering that Brother Hoyt, with whom I was acquainted, had a sawmill somewhere in these mountains, I determined to go there. I told the people at the ranch that if they would take me to Brother Hoyt's, he would take me to my father. This one of the men did.

When we got to the mill, we found Sister Hoyt and three little children alone. The men were a mile or two away cutting timber. She explained to me that the bishop had sent word for all the women folks to be moved into town as the Indians were threatening an outbreak. Some white men, it seemed, had killed an Indian, and they had sworn that they would kill ten white men for revenge. Sister Hoyt concluded her story by saying, "Yes, we are all ready to go to town tomorrow morning, and you can go with us."

She had two bake-kettles on the coals, in which two nice loaves of bread were baking. We sat there chatting without a thought of danger. I was just telling her the Nephi news when the children ran in frightened and screaming. "Oh, mother, there is a band of Indians; they are coming right towards the house!"

There they were, mounted on horses and resplendent in their war paint and feathers. They were of the Navajo tribe, the very band that was making all the trouble. Well, there was nothing for us to do but face the situation. We were two weak women, up in a canyon with no human aid within a mile. Imagine how we felt. I offered up a constant prayer in my heart to my Heavenly Father to preserve us from what might be worse than death.

They all came in, something over a dozen fierce warriors. I thought, as they looked us over and then stood talking, "They are deciding what to do with us." All at once I thought of the bread cooking on the fire and said, "Sister Hoyt, let us take these two nice loaves of hot bread and break it up and divide it among them." She answered, "All right." We then elbowed our way through the crowd of Indians and took the hot, steaming loaves from the kettle and proceeded to break them up. The Indians in the meanwhile closely watched our every movement. We asked them if they liked molasses on their bread. "Yes," they replied. Spreading each piece with molasses, we passed them around. They were pleased and showed it in every feature. Then we gave them a drink of water and they all shook hands with us . . . and took their departure.

With what fervency we thanked our Father for his protection and deliverance! When the men came home for supper, they did not complain because they had to eat mush and milk without bread that night.

Gates, *Memorial to Elizabeth Claridge McCune*, pp. 24-25.

Biographical Sketch

EMMA RAY RIGGS McKAY

Emma Ray Riggs McKay, 93, widow of President David O. McKay, passed away on November 14, 1970, in Salt Lake City. President McKay died January 18, shortly after the couple celebrated their sixty-ninth wedding anniversary.

Little is publicly known about this remarkable woman who long stood by the President's side as his "sweetheart-wife," as he called her. She was born in Salt Lake City June 23, 1877, a daughter of O. H. and Emma Robbins Riggs.

She met David O. McKay, a young man who planned to be a schoolteacher, when he came to Salt Lake City from Huntsville to enroll at the University of Utah and rented a room at the Riggs home, which was near the university. Their courtship blossomed while they were at the university, but after David's graduation in 1897, their plans for marriage were postponed when he received a call to serve as a missionary in Great Britain. Meanwhile, Emma Ray completed her university training, graduating in 1898. They were married January 2, 1901.

Emma Ray served in the auxiliaries of the Church in Ogden, raising her family at Ogden, on the McKay farm at nearby Huntsville, and later in Salt Lake City.

After her husband was called to serve as a member of the Council of the Twelve in 1906, Sister McKay was often left home to care for their seven children (one of whom died in infancy) while he traveled on assignments.

President McKay once said to their children, "All through the years you have seen how perfectly your mother fills the picture. I want to acknowledge to you and to her, how greatly her loving devotion, inspiration, and loyal support have contributed to whatever success may be ours."

As the family grew older, Sister McKay was more and more at her husband's side. He was called as second counselor in the First Presidency at the October 1934 semiannual general conference and became President of the Church April 9, 1951. In the years of his presidency they traveled together to the continents of the earth and the islands of the sea.

Improvement Era, December 1970, p. 14.

EMMA RAY RIGGS McKAY

"To Her We Owe Our Happy Family Life"

As told by David O. McKay

Aptly it has been said that "often a woman shapes the career of husband, or brother, or son." A man succeeds and reaps the honors of public applause, when in truth a quiet little woman has made it all possible—has by her tact and encouragement held him to his best, has had faith in him when his own faith has languished, has cheered him with the unfailing assurance, "You can, you must, you will."

I need not tell you children how fittingly this tribute applies to your mother. All through the years you have seen how perfectly she fills the picture. There is not a line or a touch but is applicable. For over thirty-three years, I have realized this, and each of you has known it to a greater or lesser degree as many years as your ages indicate; but like the Scotsman who "cam' near tellin' his wife once or twice" that he loved her, we have not told mother of her loving worth and inspiration to us. . . .

I want to acknowledge to you and to her how greatly her loving devotion, inspiration, and loyal support have contributed to whatever success may be ours.

Willingly and ably she has carried the responsibility of the household.

Uncomplainingly she has economized when our means have been limited.

Always prompt with meals, she has never said an unpleasant word or even shown a frown when I have kept her waiting, sometimes for hours.

If I had to take a train at midnight or later, she would either sit up with me or lie awake to make sure that I should not oversleep.

If duty required me to leave at five o'clock in the morning, she was never satisfied unless she could prepare me a bite of breakfast before I left home.

It has been mother who remembered the birthdays and purchased the Christmas presents.

Since January 2, 1901, the happy day when she became my bride, she has never given me a single worry except when she was ill, and that has been, with few exceptions, only the responsibilities of motherhood. Thus my mind has been remarkably free to center upon the problems, cares, and requirements incident to my duties and responsibilities.

In sickness, whether it was one of you or I, her untiring attention night and day was devotion personified; her practical skill, invariably effective, and her physical endurance, seemingly unlimited. Many an ache and pain she has endured in uncomplaining silence so as not to give the least worry to the loved one to whom she was giving such tender care.

Never to this day have you heard your mother say a cross or disrespectful word. This can be said truthfully, I think, of but few women in the world.

Under all conditions and circumstances, she has been the perfect lady.

Her education has enabled her to be a true helpmate; her congeniality and interest in my work, a pleasing companion; her charm and unselfishness, a lifelong sweetheart; her unbounded patience and intelligent insight to childhood, a most devoted mother. These and many other virtues, combined with her loyalty and self-sacrificing devotion to her husband, impel me to crown her the sweetest, most helpful, most inspiring sweetheart and wife that ever inspired a man to noble endeavor.

To her we owe our happy family life and whatever success we may have achieved!

Leon Hartshorn, *Memories of Mothers* (Salt Lake City: Deseret Book Co., 1971), pp. 24-26.

EMMA RAY RIGGS McKAY

"They Should Pray for Each Other's Success"

The mutual influence of brothers and sisters may be almost incalculable. Most children feel a hesitancy about doing anything in public if parents or brothers and sisters are present. They feel conscious and worry for fear they'll not succeed, or they will not excel as they would like, or for fear they will be laughed at, which unfortunately occurs in some families. I know a little girl who at twelve years of age played her own accompaniment and sang cute little songs for company when her playmates requested her so to do. One day her older brother heard her, and when they reached home, he mimicked her singing, laughed, and taunted her with the remark, "Oh, you think people like to hear you try to sing. They are just pretending."

The little girl could seldom be coaxed to sing after that; at least, she had to know that brother was nowhere in listening distance. If mothers would teach their children that wherever they go, they should pray for each other's success, and if the one performing could feel that she is doing better because of those prayers, she would always want her family to be present at the very important time of her life when she is timid and fearful of success. What she needs is the stimulus of commendation, and this should come from the members of the same family. How happy then after difficult preparation and performance to greet the family who have nothing but encouragement and praise to offer.

Emma Ray Riggs McKay, *The Art of Rearing Children Peacefully* (Brigham Young University, April 1966), p. 11.

EMMA   RAY   RIGGS   McKAY

"I Guess That Man Over There Loves You"

I accompanied my husband to a dedication of a meetinghouse in Los Angeles. We stopped on Wilshire Boulevard to get our car washed. I sat on a bench and the President was standing over by the car. Suddenly at my elbow I heard a tiny voice say, "I guess that man over there loves you." Surprised, I turned and saw a beautiful boy about seven years of age with dark curly hair and large brown eyes. "What did you say?"

"I said, I guess that man over there loves you."

"Why, yes, he loves me; he is my husband. Why do you ask?"

"Oh, 'cuz the way he smiled at you. Do you know, I'd give anything in the world if my Pop would smile at my Mom that way."

"Oh, I'm sorry he doesn't," I said.

"I guess you're not going to get a divorce, then."

"Oh, no, we're not going to get a divorce. We've been married nearly fifty years, and we are very happy. Why do you think that?"

"Oh, 'cuz everybody gets a divorce around here. My Pop is going to get a divorce from my Mom. I loved my Pop and my Mom and I"—his voice broke and tears welled in his eyes, but he was too much of a little man to let them fall.

Then he came very close and whispered confidentially in my ear, "You'd better hurry out of Los Angeles, or you'll get a divorce, too." And he picked up his papers and shuffled down the sidewalk.

My heart has bled ever since for that sweet little kiddie, and for all the other youngsters who must suffer because of the nonsensical quarrels of their parents. Mutual tolerance is indeed what we all need.

McKay, *The Art of Rearing Children Peacefully,* p. 10.

EMMA RAY RIGGS McKAY

"I Saw His Face Light Up"

Children respond favorably to praise. Let me give you an example. The first and only year I taught school, the principal came into my room the first day, which was midyear, and, pointing out a child twelve years of age, he said, before the whole roomful of pupils, "You'll have to watch out for that boy; he is the worst boy in school. He drove Miss B. away by throwing a bottle of ink at her."

What a blow for the boy, and for me, too! I thought, "Now

115

Earl will show me that that record is true by being his worst. I'll try to nip it in the bud."

I wrote a little note, saying, "Earl, I think the principal was mistaken about your being a bad boy. I trust you and know you are going to help me make this room the best in school." As I walked down the aisle I slipped it to him without anyone's noticing. I saw his face light up, and afterwards his mother told me that he brought the note home and said in an excited tone, "Read this, Mother, but don't destroy it, for I want to wear it next to my heart." He was one of my best behaved boys the remainder of the year. Praise brings good results, not cruel criticism nor abuse.

McKay, *The Art of Rearing Children Peacefully*, pp. 10-11.

EMMA RAY RIGGS McKAY

"Sister McKay, Do You Need Me?"

At one time during her husband's absence, Emma Ray was in financial difficulty. She needed a sum of money to pay some obligations. She had exhausted all her resources without being able to raise the money. Finally, the night before the money was due, with tears rolling down her cheeks, she knelt by her bed and prayed with all her heart that Heavenly Father would show her a way to obtain this needed sum.

The next morning there was a knock at the door. The visitor was Brother John Hall, a member of her stake presidency. Since he had never paid a social call on her before, she was somewhat surprised to see him when she opened the door. His first words were, "Sister McKay, do you need me? When I was down at the corner, something told me to turn up this way."

"I should say I do. Won't you come in and sit down?" She then related her problem and the ways she had tried to solve it. He promptly produced his checkbook from his pocket and wrote her the needed amount.

"But, President Hall, I have no collateral, and I don't know when I can repay you."

"Never mind, David O. will see to it when he returns."

Her letters across the world, always optimistic, always encouraging, assured her missionary that he needn't worry about family affairs or his loved ones. All was well.

Relief Society Magazine; July 1967, pp. 488-89.

ELIZABETH HUNTER MURDOCK*

"Dear Lord, I Can't Stand This Food Any Longer"

Joseph and Elizabeth Murdock were sent to the Muddy Mission [in Nevada] as colonizers in the early [eighteen] sixties and endured many hardships in caring for and supporting their families and helping to establish a settlement. It was very hot in summer and their home was made mostly of woven willows. They raised hay and a great deal of grain, as many travelers passed their way and needed food for their tired animals. Their food was poor, and coarse-bran was used to make bread, and greens and roots were used for substance many times.

Elizabeth was a good, faithful woman and willing to make her sacrifice in colonizing, but worried because her children were not thriving physically. One night as she was mixing the bran bread for the morrow, the tears fell heedlessly in the dough. She felt that she could not give her children this coarse bread again. After washing her hands she walked out into the moonlight and, to use her own words, said: "Dear Lord, I can't stand this food any longer, please send us some white flour."

*Elizabeth Hunter Murdock was born April 17, 1837. Married to Joseph Stacy Murdock, she was the mother of eleven children.

118

At three A.M. a team stopped outside their house and a man asked if he could buy feed for his horses. The sand was deep and his load was heavy and he needed feed badly. Joseph went out and gave him all the hay and oats he wanted and stood in the moonlight with his hands full of money as the man started to drive away. Just then he thought of his hungry family and called to the man and asked him what he had on his wagon. The man answered, "White flour, and anyone can have all he wants for what it cost me, as it is too heavy to pull all the way to California."

Elizabeth could hardly believe her eyes as she saw bag after bag of flour stacked in her bedroom. The next morning all the neighbors were happy too. There were hot biscuits for breakfast.

Carter, *Heart Throbs of the West,* vol. 10, p. 174.

CATHERINE A. CARLING PORTER*

"That Which God Hath Brought Together"

We were living in Holladay [Utah] in 1912 after we came out of Mexico. I was asked to be an assistant class teacher to the senior class in the YWMIA. I did not feel capable, but they said all they wanted was my consent— they knew I could do the work. I said I would do my best.

We were expected to be at the stake tabernacle for the monthly stake preparation meeting. The meeting was the next night. It had only been a short time since we came from Mexico, and my husband had gone to Nevada to get a job at a mine and

---

*Catherine Aurelia Carling Porter was born January 26, 1865, in Fillmore, Utah, a daughter of Isaac Van Wagoner and Asenath Elizabeth Browning Carling. Since her parents had little money and it was necessary for them to pay the schoolteacher for her schooling, Catherine had only a few weeks of formal schooling. At the age of twelve she moved with her family to Orderville to participate in the United Order. At a young age she was married to Edson D. Porter in the St. George Temple.

The Porters spent some twenty years in Colonia Diaz and Colonia Juarez, Mexico; they were driven out of that country in 1912. They then lived in Utah and in Arizona.

Sister Porter had thirteen children, four of whom died in infancy. She was active in the Church, teaching a religion class, Sunday School, YLMIA, and Relief Society, and served as president of three auxiliaries—YLMIA, Relief Society, and Primary. She was an ordinance worker in the Mesa Temple for twelve years and did extensive genealogical work. She died in 1957.

120

hadn't yet sent any money home, so I felt justified in staying home the night of the meeting. I would have to get the street car and go into Salt Lake City, than transfer to another car and go to the Granite Stake House. It cost the price of three car fares each way, and I had to walk about a mile to get to the street car and walk that distance after getting back. We had very little to go on, so I thought I'd better not spend it on something I thought I didn't need. I went to bed and slept till just before daybreak, when I was awakened with a shock. I thought I was in a place where there was just one building in sight. There was a large wheel attached to a shaft going through the wall. The building looked like it was built of concrete and was round with a flat top. A large, fine-looking man stood facing me, and no one else was in sight. He looked as if his message was just for me. He put forth his hand to turn the wheel, and as he did so he said in very emphatic words, "That which God hath brought together let no man put asunder."

Those words went through me like a bolt of thunder, which shook my whole being. I rose up in bed and said to myself, "What has caused such terrible shock to come to me?" Then like a flash the interpretation came to me. As he had turned that wheel I could hear a sound all through that building like fine machinery running in perfect order. That was a representation of the Church of Jesus Christ. I had given my word that I would be one who represented a part of that machinery which caused the perfect workings in the church to which I belonged. When the workers fail to take their part, it would have a tendency to tear asunder "that which God hath brought together." Those words have since been an anchor to my soul.

Elda P. Mortenson, *Isaac V. Carling Family History*, vol. 2, pp. 507-508.

LYDIA KNUDSEN RAWSON*

"Of Course I Don't Read the Poems!"

As a result of an emergency tele-
phone call, my sister and I, after several hours of flying time,
found ourselves walking down the corridor of the San Gabriel
Community Hospital to our mother's room. Our brother greeted
us. Mother did not know we were there.

All night she was restless and occasionally muttered in
tones barely audible. Toward morning she started to speak more
clearly. As we listened, we could hear the words of the twenty-
third Psalm: "The Lord is my shepherd; I shall not want."

We leaned over to hear. . . .

"Yea, though I walk through the valley of the shadow . . ."
She was repeating the Psalm and it was word perfect. By the
time she came to the last line, "I will dwell in the house of the
Lord forever," the words were completely understandable. She

*Lydia Knudsen Rawson was born in Provo, Utah, on July 31, 1880, a daughter
of Andrew and Chasty Sward Knudsen. She was married to William Dixon Rawson on
June 7, 1911; he died in 1959. She was graduated from Brigham Young Academy and
taught school in Provo and Wallsburg, Utah. Long active in Relief Society, she was a
member of the first stake board of the Los Angeles Stake Relief Society and was still
teaching a Relief Society class when she became ill at age 88. She and her husband are
parents of three children, one son and two daughters.

turned to us and smiled. Her mind seemed to clear. Her eyes brightened. She knew we were with her.

As we left the hospital later that day, we were deeply moved. It was the first time in her eighty-eight years that Mother had been seriously ill. The doctors were as surprised as we that she had rallied.

As we talked together, my brother, sister, and I, memories of our childhood came flooding back. Paramount in our reminiscences was the awareness of our mother's purity of thought. How typical that she should repeat the twenty-third Psalm!

Vivid in our memories was Mother busying herself about the house reciting a favorite poem or giving a special thought or bit of scripture that especially appealed to her. Mother not only read voraciously; she memorized. As she read she always had pencil and paper nearby, and when she found something that appealed to her, she wrote it down, not to be filed away but to be memorized. As children we were not as enthused as she about "learning things by heart," but nevertheless it was required of us. We did not just wash dishes in our house, we washed dishes and committed to memory the special thought tacked over the sink. The same memorization was required when we ironed. Part of our training in "elocution" involved reciting in front of the mirror in the bathroom so we could master the proper gestures and facial expressions.

Mother was active in Relief Society for forty-eight consecutive years. Most of that time she taught theology and literature. Teaching meant giving the lesson as outlined, *plus* memorizing all the scripture or literary works offered. . . .

Mother was never an onlooker on life. On the contrary she was always in the middle of it. When she was in her late seventies and alone, my brother built her a lovely little house at the rear of his home. She went there to live, but she refused to settle down to being an old lady. Relief Society in her new ward needed her and she needed them, she would say.

One day several years after Mother moved to her little home, my sister-in-law found her crumpled on the lawn where she had collapsed while hanging out some clothes. She was hurrying to get her washing done so she could go visiting teaching with her partner.

Later, when the doctors examined her at the hospital, she asked: "Will I be able to go home in a week? I'm scheduled to give a lesson in my church next Wednesday."

She was the visiting teacher message leader at the time. The fact that she was then eighty-eight years old, and that perhaps her body was beginning to fail, did not dawn on her. Her illness was more serious than she had thought.

Mother will be ninety next July. At the time of my last visit, she was elated because her camp of the Daughters of the Pioneers had transferred their meeting place to her convalescent home so she could share in the lessons with them.

"Can you hear the lessons as they give them, Mother?" I asked.

"No, I can't hear them because my hearing is almost gone, but that doesn't matter. You see, I've been asked to give a poem at each meeting and that is such a joy to me."

"But, Mother," I said, "how can you read a poem when your eyes are so dim?"

I should have known better than to ask that question.

"Of course I don't read the poems! One of the ladies here helps me and I memorize them."

"You memorize a new poem for each monthly meeting?"

"Certainly," she answered. "I surely can't remain here and do nothing!"

Bless you, Mother, for making your life a thing of beauty. It is a privilege to hold your hand and know that through you there is a link with a marvelous pioneer heritage. Through you we have seen life lived from barefoot days on sandy country roads to the footprints of man on the moon. It has been a beautiful journey because always you have looked beyond the clouds to see the glory of each sunrise.

Aline R. Pettit, "A Beautiful Journey," *Relief Society Magazine*, May 1970, pp. 324-28.

Biographical Sketch

LUCILE C. READING

Lucile Cardon Reading was born at Logan, Utah, to Rebecca Ann Ballard and Louis Samuel Cardon. She was one of a family of eight children. A graduate of Logan High School, she was active in school affairs, a student body officer and a member of the debating team. She continued her education at Utah State University where she was a class officer, ROTC Sponsor, president of the Women's Association and she also worked in a theater.

She married Keith E. Reading of Centerville, during 1935. They have two married sons, James C. and Don C., and four grandchildren.

She has served as a member of the general Primary presidency of the Church and is currently the managing editor of the *Friend* magazine.

Being involved seems to be a way of life for Mrs. Reading. In the past years she has been actively involved with the following community organizations: Utah State University Alumni Council, South Segamore Camp of Daughters of Utah Pioneers, LMA Club (holding at one time or another almost every office), South Davis Welfare Council, Secretary of South Davis

Chamber of Commerce, president of Davis District of Utah Federation of Women's Clubs, state officer in State Federation of Women's Clubs, member and secretary of Centerville Planning and Zoning Board, and a local PTA officer.

Her commitment to service was awarded by her being made "Woman of the Year" by the Clearfield, Layton and Bountiful chapters of Beta Sigma Phi, several years ago. She was also given an honorary Golden Gleaner from the Davis Stake and has received the "Service to Mankind" award from the Sertoma Club of Bountiful, Utah.

The experiences which have led to Mrs. Reading's present calling have been varied and continuous in service to LDS Church organizations. She served as a member of the editorial board of the *Children's Friend* as well as was a contributor to that magazine for about fourteen years.

For seven years she was a member of the Board of Trustees of the Primary Children's Hospital and is currently vice-president of the Board of Trustees of the South Davis Community Hospital.

She served as second counselor in the Primary Association from July 1962 until January 1970 and was first counselor at the time of her appointment as managing editor of the *Friend.* She is a past president of a ward Relief Society and a ward MIA, a stake board member of Davis Stake Relief Society, and taught for many years in the Relief Society, MIA, Sunday School and Primary. Continuing with graduate studies, she has done work in children's literature at the University of Utah and BYU.

Keith and Lucile Reading live in Centerville in an old stone house of charming antiquity built in 1863 and recently remodeled and restored. Brother Reading was born in the house.

Brother Keith Reading has been ill for several years and for the past two years has been bedfast. A nurse cares for him while Sister Reading is at work and on assignments. Sister Reading has now limited her civic activities so that she may take care of her husband during the evenings and on weekends. He maintains a marvelously cheerful, courageous, and supportive attitude.

LUCILE C. READING

"Fire! Fire!"

"Fire! Fire!" The warning cry brought fear to the hearts of all those who heard it in the little community of Farmington, Utah, for it usually meant complete destruction of whatever was burning.

At the first cry, Aurelia,[1] who had just arrived in Farmington to visit, ran toward the house from which smoke was billowing up into the hot August air. There was no equipment in Farmington to fight fires, so men, women, and children had already formed a line and were passing buckets of water from the creek to the burning building.

Aurelia hurriedly found a place in the water line. She was shocked to see the flames pouring out of the house, which belonged to her special friends with whom she often stayed. Earlier that summer Aurelia had rented her own house in Farmington and had moved to Salt Lake City, fifteen miles to the south. But often she returned to Farmington to "see after things and put up fruit for the winter."

---

[1] Aurelia S. Rogers, who organized the first Primary in the Church.

As Aurelia passed the heavy buckets of water along the line, she thought of her friends' loss before she thought of her own. In the upstairs bedroom where she usually slept, she had left some clothes hanging in the closet. Then with a sick feeling she remembered she had also left the Primary record books on a table close to a window. These books contained the history of the very first Primary ever organized.

"I mourned exceedingly," said Aurelia later. "I would not have minded losing my clothes (I had a nice plush cape, a dress, and some other things burned) if the records could only have been saved."

Aurelia was heartsick as she returned to her home in Salt Lake after helping her friends move into a nearby vacant house. But the loss of the record books haunted her, and in a few days she visited Farmington again to gather information so she could write another history of the organization of the Primary.

What thrilling news awaited her there! These are her very own words telling what she learned about her records:

> Brother Moroni Secrist, who was bishop of our ward at the time, felt prompted to climb onto the porch and go through the window to my room, thinking he might save some of the property; but when he went inside, the smoke was so dense he was nearly suffocated and had to be helped out by others who had followed. As he neared the window, he reached out his hand and felt the cover on the table and drew it toward him, gathering up the corners with the books and a box of notions that I had, and passed them to those on the outside. Thus the records were saved through the Providence of God.

The organization of Primary took place just ninety years ago this month [August 1868], and Aurelia Rogers' rescued history is even more precious today.

Children's Friend, August 1968, p. 15.

"Night Ride"

Nearly everyone in the coach was asleep. A little girl, her eyes closed, sat listening to the sounds of the train as it rushed through the soft spring night. She heard, too, the noise of sleeping passengers and the restless stirring of those in the car who could not seem to get comfortable.

Suddenly her keen ears caught another sound. Someone was crying. Then there came the murmur of voices. Soon afterward an excited woman hurried down the aisle of the car. She bent over each sleeping passenger and asked in a loud whisper, "Are you a minister?" Finally she called out, "A woman back here wants a prayer. Is there a preacher in this car?" No one answered; no one offered to help.

The little girl waited until the woman was near her seat. Then she reached up a small hand to stop her and said, "I can pray. Will I do?" By this time the woman was desperate. "Follow me," she answered. "I guess you're better than no one."

"You'll have to take my arm," replied the girl, "I can't see."

The woman took the hand of the little girl and led her to the end of the car. She explained that a woman who was in the ladies' lounge had a great sorrow, that she couldn't stop crying, and that she had asked for a prayer. "And," confessed the woman, "I don't know what to say to comfort her and I've forgotten how to pray."

The crying woman did not hear the woman and the little girl until they were by her side. She looked up through her tears as she saw a child's hand reach out for hers. Then a sweet voice began, "Our Father which art in heaven. . . ."

When the prayer was finished, the tearful woman wiped her eyes and stood up. There were tears now in the eyes of the other woman, too. The little girl smiled at them both. Even though she could not see, she knew they smiled back at her.

Children's Friend, May 1963, p. 24.

LUCILE C. READING

"Madeline's Dream"

Madeline, her clothes under her arms, ran down the stairs and into the kitchen where her mother was preparing breakfast. Mother looked up to say good morning to her little girl, but when she saw how pale and breathless Madeline was, she asked, "What's the matter? Are you sick?"

"No," answered Madeline, but at the moment she could say no more. She sank down onto a stool near the fireplace and stared into the flame. She wondered how she could ever put into words the strange dream she had just had, and what her mother would think if she could.

It had seemed in her dream that she was a young lady sitting on a small strip of meadow close to the vineyard and that as she watched to make sure the goats didn't tramp on the vines and eat them, she glanced down at a Sunday School book in her lap. As she looked up again, she was startled to see three strange men.

At the remembrance, Madeline shivered in fright, just as she had shivered in her dream. But almost at once there came the feeling of peace that had flooded over her when one of the men said, "Don't be frightened. We have come from a place far from here to tell you about the true and everlasting gospel."

Then the men told her that an angel had directed a boy to find an important book of gold hidden in the earth. They said that someday she, Madeline, would be able to read this book, and then, because of it, she would gladly leave her home, cross the great ocean, and go to America to live.

In the warm, sweet-smelling kitchen Madeline relived her dream. It seemed so real to her that she turned pale again and began to tremble. Father came in from milking the goats and asked, just as her mother had done, "What's the matter? Are you sick?"

Madeline could only shake her head. Father gently stooped down beside her, picked up a stocking, and without another word began to help her dress. Afterward he lifted her onto his lap and quietly asked, "Do you want to tell me about it?"

Madeline nodded. It was hard to get the words started, but then they seemed to tumble over each other in their eagerness to be spoken. Mother left her preparations for their simple breakfast of figs, potatoes, and goat milk so she could hear every amazing detail of the dream. Father listened intently, occasionally nodding his head as if he understood more than was being said.

That night when the family gathered around the fireplace for the evening prayer, Father told again the story of why they lived in a small village high in the north Italian Alps. Their grandparents many generations back had had homes in the lovely valleys at the foot of these lofty mountains. There the people lived simple happy lives, basing all they did on the teachings of the apostles who had lived at the time of Christ. The Vaudois (meaning people who live in the valleys of the Alps) even sent forth missionaries two by two to teach. Many people from other lands were converted to their faith.

News of their success reached Rome, and word went to the Vaudois valleys that they must give up their own church and abide by the dictates of the larger ruling church in Rome. This they refused to do. In fact, the Vaudois clung with even greater faith to the authority and teachings of the New Testament as handed down to them.

Angered, Pope Innocent VIII proclaimed a general crusade for the extermination of every member of the Vaudois church.

Soon the peaceful valleys where they lived were filled with tragedy and destruction. There was hardly a rock that did not mark a scene of death. Those who survived were driven from their homes. They retreated higher and ever higher up the steep mountains.

The many years of unbelievable suffering resulted in the deaths of all but three hundred members of the Vaudois church. These people settled high in the Piedmont valleys of the Alps, their villages seeming to cling to the mountainsides. They were surrounded by inaccessible crags and cliffs.

It was hard to eke out a living. Each spring the women and children went down the steep mountains and in baskets carried the soil that had been washed down in the winter storms back up to their terraced fields and gardens. But in these craggy mountains they were quite isolated, and here they raised their hands to the sky and solemnly swore to defend their homes and their religion to the death, as their fathers had done before them.

Madeline's family had heard this story many times, but they never tired of it. Even the youngest children thrilled to hear of the courage of their tall, strong grandparents. The older children often expressed gratitude for their home and for their church with its motto "The Light Shining in Darkness."

Long after everyone else was asleep that night, Madeline could hear the murmur of her parents' voices. The last thing she remembered before she went to sleep was hearing her mother insist, "But we already have the true gospel, so there couldn't be any real meaning to that story Madeline told us."

Madeline did not hear her father's answer, but occasionally as the years went by, he would question her concerning her dream. Even though some of the details became vague to her, they never did to him.

About eight years after Madeline's dream, the king of Sardinia, pressured by England and other countries to stop persecuting the Piedmont protestants, granted his Vaudois subjects freedom of religion. The tragic 800-year war ended in February 1848.

The very next year Lorenzo Snow, who later became the fifth president of the Church, was called to open a mission in

Italy. But he and his two companions could not find anyone interested in their message. Discouraged, he wrote, "I see no possible means of accomplishing our object. All is darkness."

On September 18, 1850, Lorenzo Snow and his two companions climbed a high mountain in northern Italy and on a large projecting rock offered a fervent prayer for guidance. They were then inspired to dedicate the land for the preaching of the gospel, and they named the rock upon which they stood "The Rock of Prophecy."

Before leaving the mountain, the missionaries sang "The Hymn of the Vaudois Mountaineers in Times of Persecution." The strains of this song had floated down into the valleys many times from high caves and fissures in the rocks where the persecuted had been hiding. It had been a rallying cry as the Vaudois took up arms to fortify their mountain passes. It had been sung in thanksgiving in their church services. Now the three missionaries, standing on The Rock of Prophecy, sang the stirring words:

For the strength of the hills we bless thee,
Our God, our fathers' God;
Thou hast made thy children mighty
By the touch of the mountain sod.

Shortly afterward, on a Saturday afternoon, Madeline's father went home early from his work of building a chimney for a neighbor. He told his family that three strangers were coming to bring an important message. "I must dress in my best clothes and go welcome them," he said.

He found the men he was looking for on Sunday morning and invited them to go home with him. As they walked up over the winding paths and through the dangerously narrow mountain passes, Madeline's father told them of the dream his daughter had had many years before.

When they reached his small rock home, they found Madeline sitting on a little strip of meadow close to the vineyard. She looked up from the Sunday School book she was reading into the faces of three men. They told her they had come to give her people the message contained in a wonderful book of gold that had been taken out of the earth, and said that she could now read this book.

That evening Madeline's neighbors came to meet the strangers and hear their message. Some of the men found it so unusual and exciting that they stayed up all night to learn more about the newly revealed truths that had been brought to them by these missionaries of The Church of Jesus Christ of Latter-day Saints.

Some baptisms were held in October 1850. Twenty families eventually accepted the gospel, and as Madeline's dream became a reality, the Vaudois area truly became "A Light Shining in Darkness."

Friend, November 1971, pp. 2-4.

LUCILE   C.   READING

"Summer Storm"

The rounded thunderhead billowed up in the southwest. Rachel watched it and shivered when she saw a far-off flash of lightning and heard the low rumble of thunder. She was alone and terrified.

Rachel knew her older sisters and mother would probably be nervous too if they were home. But even a half-fearful family would be some comfort, she thought. She didn't expect anyone back for several hours, and wished again that she had gone with her sisters. Why had she stayed home just to finish reading a book?

Most of all Rachel thought of her father, as she anxiously watched the fast-moving black clouds. She had often wondered why he always sat on the front porch during a summer storm. Several times he had invited her and others in the family to join him. He seemed to want company, but Rachel had always been too frightened to go outside—and she guessed her sisters and mother must have been too.

A gusty wind began to bend the trees. Rachel jumped as a window in an upstairs room banged shut. The first big drops of rain splashed down just as Father drove into the driveway, jumped out, and ran into the house.

Rachel's heart turned over with a suffocating love for him as he explained, "Thought I'd better check on you. How about a ringside seat for an A-number-one attraction tonight?"

Rachel reluctantly followed her father out onto the porch. He pulled two chairs close together and then reached out and took one of Rachel's trembling hands and held it tight.

"How beautiful this all is," he said softly. "Nature's fireworks! You know, being frightened won't ever stop a storm, but facing the beauty and majestic power of it can bring a strange and exciting kind of joy—and a deep gratitude for being a part of such a wondrous world. People miss so much in life if they spend all their time being afraid."

Hearing his quiet words, Rachel relaxed a bit and she looked up. She let her eyes sweep across the sky as one streak of lightning followed another and thunder growled and crashed around them. In all of her ten years she had never really seen a summer storm before. It is beautiful, she thought.

That moment, with her father's hand tightly holding hers, Rachel decided that all of her life she'd be glad for the beauty in the world and she would try to have courage—even in a storm.

Children's Friend, August 1969, p. 23.

LUCILE C. READING

"President Smith Took Him by the Hand"

Eleven-year-old John Roothoof lived in Rotterdam, Holland. He had once been happy going to school and church, playing with his friends, and doing all the things a boy enjoys. Then without warning, a painful eye disease caused him to lose his sight. No longer could he go to school or read. He could not even see well enough to play with his friends. Each day was filled with darkness and suffering.

Word reached the Latter-day Saints in Holland that President Joseph F. Smith would visit them. John thought about this for a long time, and then he said to his mother, "The prophet has the most power of any missionary on earth. If you'll take me with you to the meeting so he can look into my eyes, I believe I'll be healed."

At the close of the meeting the next Sunday, President Smith went to the back of the small chapel to greet the people and shake hands with each one. Sister Roothoof helped John, his eyes bandaged, go with the others to speak to their beloved leader. President Smith took him by the hand and then with great tenderness lifted the bandages and looked into John's pain-filled eyes. He blessed the boy and promised him he would see again.

Arriving home, John's mother took the bandages from his eyes so she could bathe them as the doctors had told her to do. As she did so, John cried out with joy, "Oh, Mamma, my eyes are well. I can see fine now—and far too. And I can't feel any pain!"

Friend, August 1973, p. 36.

138

Biographical Sketch

Sarah de Arman Pea Rich was born September 23, 1814, at Looking Glass Prairie, Illinois, to John and Elizabeth Knighton Pea. She was baptized into the Church on December 15, 1835, the first of her father's family to receive the fullness of the gospel. Her father, mother, and sister soon followed her example.

She married Charles C. Rich, who later became an apostle, on February 11, 1838, at Far West, Missouri. It was here that she first became acquainted with the Prophet Joseph Smith. Sister Rich gave birth to her first child and daughter on March 4, 1839. The child was given her name by Patriarch Joseph Smith, Sen., who also blessed Sister Rich, promising that she should live to a good old age.

In November 1839 the family moved to Nauvoo, and when the Prophet organized the female Relief Society in 1842, Sister Rich became an active member.

When the revelation on plural marriage was revealed to her, though it was originally one of the greatest trials to befall her, she decided to accept this order and gave her consent for her husband to enter this covenant.

141

After the Nauvoo Temple was finished both she and her husband were called to do ordinance work in it. They continued work here until the exodus of the Saints from Nauvoo in 1846. They left Winter Quarters in June 1847 and arrived in the Salt Lake Valley on October 3.

In 1862 Elder Rich was called to colonize the Bear Lake Valley in northern Utah. Sister Rich went with him and resided there for three years until the severe climate necessitated her return to the Salt Lake Valley. However, when Brother Rich was stricken with paralysis in 1880 she returned to Bear Lake Valley to be with him and nurse him.

The mother of six sons and three daughters, she was a teacher in the Relief Society in her Salt Lake ward from the time of its first organization until her death on September 12, 1893.

Andrew Jenson, *LDS Biographical Encyclopedia,* pp. 207-11.

SARAH PEA RICH

"I Think I Should Be Happy to Get a Good Companion"

Following her [Sarah Pea's] conversion, the missionaries expressed grave concern lest she should fall in love with an outsider and marry one not of the faith. They cautioned her as well as her unmarried sister. One of the elders said to Sarah one day, "I have taken the liberty of recommending you to a very fine young man, who I believe would make you a good companion."

A few months later another missionary, while talking to the family about gathering to Missouri, said to Sarah, "I have a good young elder picked out for you." To the surprise of all he proved to be the same one whom the former elder had so highly recommended to her. This caused no end of teasing and bantering at Sarah's expense.

A few weeks later the elders who had baptized the family returned for a visit; and one of them said to Sarah, "While I was in Kirtland, I recommended you to a very worthy young man, who is an elder in the Church; and when I told him of you, he said, 'That same girl has been recommended to me twice before, and now I must hunt her up!' " Sarah was very much astonished when, on inquiring his name, she heard the same name that had been twice before recommended to her. She makes this comment: "We all wondered, thinking how strange this should be!"

About a month after this last conversation, Sarah received a letter postmarked St. Louis, Missouri. Imagine her surprise when she read:

Miss Sarah Pea:

It is with pleasure that I at this time pen a few lines to you, although a perfect stranger to you. However, I trust that these few lines may be received by you, and may be the beginning of a happy acquaintance with you.

I will now let you know the reason for my boldness in writing to you. It is because Elder G. M. Hinkle and others have highly recommended you as a saint of the last days, as being worthy of my attention.

I think I should be happy to get a good companion such a one as could take comfort with through life, and such a one as could take comfort with me. As you have been recommended to me as such, I should be very happy to see you and converse with you on the subject. . . .

When this comes to hand and after you read and meditate upon it, I should be glad if you would write me an answer to it. . . .

Yours with the best of respects,
Charles C. Rich

After reading this extraordinary message, Sarah pondered deeply upon her answer. She began thinking more seriously of marriage. What should she do about it? She prayed over her problem, for she couldn't help but believe that "the hand of the Lord" was in it. She had always prayed that she might be led by the Spirit of the Lord in the selection of a companion for life, and now, as never before, she wanted him to guide her. . . .

The next step Sarah took was to go to God's word, the Bible, for help. She had been reared a Methodist; so, as John Wesley was wont to do whenever he was perplexed, she took down the family Bible, closed her eyes, flipped open the pages at random, and placed her finger upon a verse. Opening her eyes, she read the words under her finger. There, sure enough, was her answer, as plain as the words before her. She immediately took paper, pen and ink and wrote her answer:

Mr. Charles C. Rich:

"Intreat me not to leave thee, or to return from following after thee; for whither thou goest, I will go; and where thou lodgest, I will lodge: thy people shall be my people, and thy God my God: Where thou diest, will I die, and there will I be buried: the Lord do so to me, and more also, if ought but death part thee and me."

With great respect, I remain
Yours truly,
Sarah Pea

Six and a half months transpired before Sarah met Charles, but they met and were not disappointed. Four months after their meeting they were married.

Ivan J. Barrett, "Heroines of the Church," Brigham Young University Education Week Lectures, 1956, pp. 9-12.

SARAH PEA RICH

"The Spirit Tells Me You Are Out of Money"

One day a woman came to see the President [Rich]. The wife of one of the Battalion boys, she told him with copious tears that she had nothing for her children to eat. This was before any government money had come into the community through the soldiers. I shall let Mrs. Rich tell the story:

My husband turned to me and said, "Let this Sister have some flour, Sarah." This was a puzzle to me, knowing that we did not have twenty pounds of flour in the house, and none in the place to buy, even if we had the money to buy it with. So I said, "We haven't twenty pounds of flour in the house and none that can be bought." He looked at me and smiled. "Sarah," he said, "let her have all that there is in the house, and trust in the Lord to provide for us."

I did as he bade me, but wondered how our own children

were to eat. When the sister was gone, Mr. Rich said, "I know, Sarah, that the Lord will open the way for us to live. So don't feel uneasy." I too began to ask the Lord to open the way for us.

Along toward the evening we saw some covered wagons coming down the hill toward the house. They stopped in front, and the men came in. One of them proved to be Brother Sidwell, who had been with Brother Benson and who had called on us in the East. Brother Sidwell said he wanted to stop with us over night, and my husband told him he could. He then turned to Mr. Rich and said to him, "The Spirit tells me you are out of money, and tells me to help you." And he handed Mr. Rich fifty dollars. Mr. Rich handed the money to me, saying, "Now you see the Lord has opened the way for us to get flour." He was overcome with gratitude.

With understanding our situation, Brother Sidwell informed us that "we have enough bread in our wagons for tonight and the morning." He told us also they had a wagon load of flour a little way back, which would reach here either tonight or in the morning, so that we might be supplied with breadstuff.

On this we burst into tears, to think the Lord had so blessed us for our kindness to the poor sister and her children.

When the wagon load of flour arrived, Mr. Rich not only laid in a supply for ourselves, but got a lot to give out to others that were sick and poor in the place. The man with the flour also let us have some groceries. He was a wealthy bachelor on his way to Winter Quarters. When, later on, we went to Winter Quarters to begin our journey to the West, he assisted us and others to start to the mountains.

John Henry Evans, *Charles Coulson Rich: Pioneer Builder of the West* (New York: The Macmillan Company, 1936), pp. 125-26.

RHODA RICHARDS*

"I Never Was an Idler"

Some of our ambitious little girls
and working women would doubtless be interested in a simple
sketch of some few things which I have accomplished by manual
labor. When myself and my sisters were only small girls, our
excellent mother taught us how to work, and in such a wise manner did she conduct our home education that we always loved to
work, and were never so happy as when we were most usefully
employed. We knit our own and our brothers' stockings, made
our own clothes, braided and sewed straw hats and bonnets,
carded, spun, wove, kept house, and did everything that girls
and women of a self-sustaining community would need to do.

The day that I was thirteen years old I wove thirteen yards
of cloth; and in twenty months, during which time I celebrated
my eightieth birthday, I carded twenty weight of cotton, spun
215 balls of candle-wicking and 200 run of yarn, prepared for
the weaver's loom; besides doing my housework, knitting socks,
and making shirts for "my boys" (some of the sons of my

*Rhoda Richards was born August 8, 1784, at Hopkisstar, Massachusetts. She was
the sister of Willard Richards, who served in the Council of the Twelve and also the First
Presidency, and of Phineas and Levi Richards.

brothers). I merely make mention of these things as samples of what my lifework has been. I never was an idler, but have tried to be useful in my humble way, "doing what my hands found to do with my might."

I now begin to feel the weight of years upon me, and can no longer do as I have done in former years for those around me; but, through the boundless mercies of God, I am still able to wash and iron my own clothes, do up my lace caps, and write my own letters. My memory is good, and as a general thing I feel well in body and mind. I have witnessed the death of many near and dear friends, both old and young. In my young days I buried my first and only love, and true to that affiance, I have passed companionless through life; but am sure of having my proper place and standing in the resurrection.

Tullidge, *The Women of Mormondom*, pp. 421-22.

Biographical Sketch

ANN EVERINGTON ROBERTS

Ann Everington Roberts was born in Norfolk, England. Since her parents were both dead, she supported herself by working in a shop where she trimmed hats and did fine stitching for the grand ladies of the countryside.

When she was 21 she met a young blacksmith, named Ben Roberts. They were married June 15, 1848. Several children were born to them. She was converted to the Church. Her constant prayer was that her husband would be converted also. He was baptized, but he was ever lukewarm, and later she was separated from him.

Ann had an insatiable desire to go to America to take her little brood to Zion where they would be numbered among the "chosen people," and her sons would have the opportunities of a new land. But Ben refused to consider such a move, and the breach grew wider and wider between them.

After the absence of several months, Ben sent Ann a sum of money. She decided to use this money as part payment on her passage to Utah. It took more than five months to reach Utah, and the trek across the plains had to be made before the cold weather began.

It was impossible for Ann to take her entire family with her. Mary, now twelve, was left in the care of some distant relatives. She left her five-year-old son Henry[1] with some members of the branch. She took Annie and Thomas, the baby, with her.

It was a long, hard journey—many weeks on a sailing vessel, where the baby contracted "ship fever." Before she reached the mountains, the baby died. A simple service was said over the little grave, and with leadened feet and heavy heart she continued the journey. Upon reaching Utah, she settled in Bountiful and started to do sewing. When she had saved enough money to bring her children to Utah, she sent for them.

Adah Roberts Naylor, *Relief Society Magazine*, January 1934, pp. 3-8.

[1]Brigham H. Roberts, who later became a member of the First Council of the Seventy.

ANN EVERINGTON ROBERTS

"He Was Speaking of America"

One night as she [Ann Everington Roberts] passed through the streets, she was attracted by a gathering of people on one of the busy corners. A man was singing in a clear tenor voice, the song ended, and Ann paused a moment; he was speaking of America. "A land blessed above all other lands"—"A land of liberty—Where Zion is to be built in the tops of the mountains"—"A Zion unto which all people shall gather." She stopped for a while and listened and then passed on, somewhat troubled in her mind about "the gathering of Israel" which the speaker had described. She sat up late that night reading her Bible and pondering in her heart the words she had heard.

The next evening Ann made herself ready and went out in search of the street preacher. This time she waited until he had finished speaking, then talked with him and obtained some of his literature, which she carried home and carefully studied. She tried to interest her husband in this new faith—this new Zion, this new-old gospel of the brotherhood of man—but he would listen to none of it. And so it was that she went alone and was baptized a member of The Church of Jesus Christ of Latter-day Saints.

Relief Society Magazine, January 1934, pp. 3-4.

ANN   EVERINGTON   ROBERTS

"A Wooden Breadbox"

Ben sent Ann a sum of money. She decided to use this money as part payment on her passage to Utah. The decision was made hurriedly, as it was now April and the last company of Saints to leave that year was to sail May 2. It took more than five months to reach Utah, and the trek across the plains had to be made before the cold weather began.

It was impossible for Ann to take her entire family with her. Mary, now twelve years old, was left in the care of some distant relatives by the name of Pie, who operated a factory where china was burned and decorated. It was agreed that she should work as an apprentice for her board and keep. A Brother and Sister Tovey had recently joined the branch, coming up from Scotland where they had embraced the gospel. Little was known about them, but Ann felt that anyone who had become a Latter-day Saint was to be believed in and trusted, and so it was that she left behind, in charge of this couple, her five-year-old son Henry. Annie and Thomas, the baby, she took with her.

It was a long, hard journey—many weeks on a sailing vessel, where the baby contracted "ship fever"—then torturous days in railroad cars, and then the long tramp across the plains. Little Thomas was very ill now, wasted away by the fever to almost a skeleton. Ann carried him in her arms as she trudged

154

along beside the covered wagon train. Before she reached the mountains he died, and for the first time, Ann's all-but-dauntless courage failed her. She could not endure the thought of placing in the ground the body of the little son for whom she had visioned so splendid a future. It was Horten Haight, captain of the company, who came to her rescue. Taking from his wagon a wooden bread box, he improvised a coffin and helped Ann prepare the tiny body for burial. A simple service was said over the little grave, and with leadened feet and a heavy heat she continued the journey.

Upon reaching Utah Ann went immediately to a small settlement eight miles north from Salt Lake City, known as Bountiful. Here she had friends—Saints she had known in England—and here she opened a shop where she made hats and did sewing and tailor'ng, hoping thereby to not only support herself and daughter Annie, but to accumulate enough money to bring her children to Utah.

Relief Society Magazine, January 1934, pp. 5-6.

ANN EVERINGTON ROBERTS

" 'Promise Me,' She Had Said"

Ann was blessed with an abundance of vitality, and she worked early and late, often sewing far into the night, in her struggle to get warm clothing, bedding, and money enough to send for her children, but nearly three years had passed before she had accomplished her purpose. The clothing and bedding were sent to New York, the money to England, and Mary, now a girl of fifteen, was prepared for the journey, but no trace of the boy Henry could be found.

And so it was that a great search was set up in the branches of the Mormon Church throughout the British Isles.

The Toveys, tiring of the restrictions placed on them by the teachings of the Church, disappeared shortly after Ann left England, taking the boy Henry with them. Their sole earthly belongings were a violin, a Bible, and a bundle of clothing. It was summertime, and on foot they went through the green lanes of England. They worked a little at odd jobs and begged, and at night they slept huddled together under the hedges. But when cold weather came they sought the cities, where shelter could be had at low cost and where Mr. Tovey, who was a stonecutter by trade, would sometimes find employment.

Both Mr. and Mrs. Tovey were given to drink, and many hours were whiled away at taverns where Mr. Tovey played his violin and Mrs. Tovey sang in a cracked voice, in return for which they were given free drinks and sometimes food. They taught Henry a number of old English ballads, and he would stand on a table and entertain the patrons by singing in a sweet childish treble, afterwards passing his hat for pennies. One day some soldiers, noticing the splendid rhythm of the lad, suggested that he would make a good drummer boy for the army.

When Henry was seven the Toveys, who had now changed their name to Gailey, quarreled seriously and decided to separate. Mrs. Gailey, Henry learned from their conversation, wanted to join a brother who had recently finished a term in prison, and Mr. Gailey, not wishing to be encumbered with a small boy and evidently remembering the comment of the soldier, took him to nearby barracks where he was accepted as a drummer boy in the British Army. Measurements were taken for his uniform, and Mr. Gailey was to return with him the following day, but that night, as Henry slept, his mother's face appeared before him. She was weeping, and the promise he had made at their parting flashed into his mind. "Promise me," she had said, "that if I am unable to send for you, that you will, when you grow to be a man, go to Utah." The dream awakened him and something within him said, "If you serve in the army you will never get to Utah." He got up quietly, and taking his clothes in his arms, crept down the stairs and out into the dark street. He stopped to dress and then started on his pilgrimage back to Thorplton, where he thought he could find the elders who had known his mother.

For many weeks he wandered about, eating when he could find food and sleeping with other street urchins in empty boxes and doorways. He inquired everywhere for Mormon elders, but no one seemed to have heard of them, and so, overcome by loneliness and longing for the healing influence of the familiar, he retraced his steps back to where he had lived with the Gaileys. They welcomed him back, and life for him settled back into the old groove.

Ann Everington had been in America four long years, and Henry had passed his ninth birthday when the elders found him. He was a sturdy lad, like his mother in appearance—the same clear blue eyes with the wide setting, the same fine head line, and the same air of serious earnestness. He could neither read nor write, nor did he know the letters of the alphabet, but necessity had made him a keen observer, and he was far older than his years. He joined his sister Mary at Liverpool, and late in April 1866, they set sail for America. . . .

He slept with the other men and boys under the wagons, shivering in the cold because the bedding sent by his mother had been lost, and the only covering he had was the flannel petticoat of his sister that was dropped down to him when she went to bed inside the wagon. He was up early and out to the campfire to warm himself; he liked to watch the sun pulling itself up over the edge of the earth, for its coming meant warmth and comfort.

During the day he made tours of inspection that often led him far afield. Once he was left behind and forced to swim the Missouri River before he could rejoin the wagon train. It was there that he lost his coat and shoes, a loss that filled him with a sad foreboding. He had lovely remembrances of his mother. Her clothes made by herself, often from cast-off garments of her rich customers, had a line and a style that gave her a fine appearance, and Henry thought her very beautiful. He remembered her exactitude about clean hands, well-brushed hair, and neat clothing, and the sight of his bare bruised feet made him miserable. . . .

Along the trail they came upon a cluster of log cabins that had been burned and were still smouldering. Henry stayed behind to investigate. Sticking out between two burned logs were the . . . legs of a [dead] man, and on those legs were a practically new pair of shoes. He pulled and tugged until the shoes were free . . . then running swiftly he caught up with the train, and climbing quietly into the back of a provision wagon, he hid his precious find against the time when he should meet his mother— a great burden had been lifted from his heart.

In October they reached the Valley. As the long wagon train slowly wended its way through Emigration Canyon, Henry hurried ahead and, climbing to a high cliff, caught his first glimpse of Zion. . . .

The wagons rolled into the city streets, and at last the great moment had come. The lad rushed to the provision wagon where his treasure was hidden. They were a man's shoes, much too large for him—but they were shoes, and slipping his bruised and swollen feet into them, he marched at the head of the procession up Main Street to the Tithing Office, where his mother awaited him.

Relief Society Magazine, January 1934, pp. 7-8.

BETTY CLARK RUFF*

"My Toddler Taught Me About the Preexistence and Death"

I had always heard that one could learn many things from children, but not until we had a very precious experience with one of our own did I realize how true this could be.

This occasion took place when our first child, Alan, was just past two. Alan had learned to talk very early, so by this time he spoke very clearly and could express himself with a sizeable vocabulary for his age.

Alan's great-aunt Lida had just passed away, and I had been worrying about how I was going to tell him about death. We had

---

*Betty Clark Ruff was born at Beaver, Utah, to Hiram William and Marie McGregor Clark. The family later moved to Denver, where she was graduated from East Denver High School and was also active in the Denver Branch of the Church, especially in music, as she was trained both as an organist and pianist. She was graduated from Brigham Young University with high honors and as valedictorian of her class on June 9, 1943. On August 28, 1943, she became the wife of George Robert Ruff; they are the parents of five children, three sons and two daughters. All three sons are Eagle Scouts; the first two have served missions, and the third is planning to go soon. The family resides in the Ensign Fifth Ward in Salt Lake City.

Sister Ruff has spent her time since having a family in being a wife and mother and being active in genealogy and in the auxiliary organizations of the wards in which she has lived.

taken him to see her once or twice a week, so there had to be some explanation for the termination of our visits.

Mustering all my courage, for I was new at that sort of thing then, I sat Alan on the kitchen stool and drew up a chair. "Alan, honey," I said, "Aunt Lida has gone back to Heavenly Father."

But, before I could say anything more, he asked, "Who took her?" I stumbled around for an answer, and then I said, "It must have been someone she knew."

Immediately his little face lit up as if he recognized a familiar situation. He said with a happy smile, "Oh, I know what it's like! Grandpa Clark brought me when I came to you. He'll probably take me back when I die."

Alan then proceeded to describe his Grandfather Clark, my father, who had been dead nearly twelve years. He had never even seen a picture of him. He told me how much he loved his grandfather and how good he had been to him. He indicated that my father had helped to teach him and prepare him to come here. He also spoke of Heavenly Father as a definite memory.

Needless to say, this little conversation with Alan that I had been dreading turned out to be one of the sweetest experiences of my life. It left me limp with humility and joy. I no longer felt sorry that my father could not see my children. As each little soul has come along, I have felt that my father probably was better acquainted with the newcomer than was I. This has been great comfort to me.

Immediately after this occasion, Alan's father talked to him and Alan repeated the same answers to him. He later told the experience to his Grandmother Clark. For several months he talked about these things as a happy, natural memory of real experiences. Then, suddenly, the memory was erased and he did not know what we were talking about when we discussed it.

But, he had taught us some great truths, for which we are most thankful; and had verified the inspiration in Wordsworth's lines:

> . . . Our birth is but a sleep and a forgetting:
> The Soul that rises with us, our life's Star,
> Hath had elsewhere its setting,

And cometh from afar:
Not in entire forgetfulness,
And not in utter nakedness,
But trailing clouds of glory do we come
From God, who is our home:
Heaven lies about us in our infancy! . . .

Instructor, February 1963, p. 61.

ELLIS   REYNOLDS   SHIPP *

"I Bade Goodbye and Godspeed"

On February 24, 1867, Our Father of Love Divine bestowed upon me, His mortal child, the most gracious and sanctified gift within His storehouse of blessings. A beautiful son! A body without one blemish, endowed with a sanctified Spirit! My beautiful Baby Boy!

When that tiny precious little body was placed in my arms no mortal pen could tell my joy! Only one divine could understand the exquisite bliss of that supreme happiness. And only He the Eternal Giver could know and grant unto me the most sincere prayer of all of my life to be a perfect mother. My being seemed transported to the realms of purest, most perfect endeavor; an idealistic, heaven-inspired motherhood, in which to live for another without one instinct save to bless this supreme

---

° Ellis R. Shipp was born January 20, 1847, in Davis County, Iowa, a daughter of William F. Reynolds and Anna Hawley. She attended the Woman's Medical College of Pennsylvania and graduated in 1878 with the degree of doctor of medicine. She practiced medicine in Utah for many years. In 1910 she published a volume of poems entitled *Life Liner.* She married Milford B. Shipp on May 5, 1866, and became the mother of ten children. Dr. Shipp received many honors in life for her sixty years of unselfish service in the medical profession. She died January 31, 1939, just eleven days after her ninety-second birthday.

162

gift from heaven which seemed so truly mine; to nourish, to cherish, to rear and mould and guide unto all the highest, holiest, exalted possibilities of earthly achievement. What a sacred mission for mortal woman to fill!

When my little babe was only nine days old my husband bade us all goodbye through the call for faithful men to go across the globe to preach salvation to the world. This was not a great surprise, but still it brought us dreads and fears of what the long and weary years would bring, for England seemed so far away— miles on miles to traverse over oceans deep and broad to span.

And we were then so poor in worldly means, but yet so rich in faith! Souls o'er-filled with confidence and trust in our All-wise and heavenly Guide. Though in mortal powers weak, we had courage and the will to help the Cause of Truth and Justice. Women in those days and in all generations of time have shown their valor, loyalty, and devotion in every righteous cause. Therefore we were indeed most anxious to do all in our power to make ourselves self-sustaining that we could do our part for a cause we loved and honored.

I was still prostrate with weakness and could scarce endure the thought of parting with a devoted companion who seemed to me the ideal of all a woman's nature craved! And yet my soul desired that he, so capable to expound the Gospel Truths, should do his part completely, and that I must do my part in courage to take care of myself and precious family. So I curbed my anxious fears and in faith rejoiced that he should go to lands afar to bring to many souls the message of salvation. I felt that anything the Lord required of me I could willingly endure. Thus far in life I had willingly received and tried to live his revealed word, and with this sincere trust and hope I bade goodbye and Godspeed.

Ellis Shipp Musser, *The Early Autobiography and Diary of Ellis Reynolds Shipp, M.D.* (Salt Lake City: Deseret News Press, 1962), pp. 47, 58-59.

AMANDA SMITH *

"A Living Miracle of the Power of God"

We arrived in Caldwell County, near Haun's Mill, nine wagons of us in company. Two days before we arrived we were taken prisoners by an armed mob that had demanded every bit of ammunition and every weapon we had. We surrendered all. They knew it, for they searched our wagons.

A few miles more brought us to Haun's Mill. . . . My husband pitched his tent by a blacksmith's shop. . . . I sat in my tent. Looking up I suddenly saw the mob coming—the same that took

*Amanda Barnes Smith was born February 22, 1809, in the town of Becket, Beckshire County, Massachusetts, a daughter of Ezekiel and Fannie Barnes. While she was but a young girl she moved with her parents to Ohio, and was married at the age of 18 years.

She was a member of the Campbellite faith, together with Sidney Rigdon and others, until she heard the fullness of the gospel preached. On April 1, 1831, at the age of 22, she was baptized into the Church. Soon afterwards she moved to Kirtland, Ohio, where she assisted in building the temple, but in 1838 she and her family were forced to leave because of mob violence. From there they went to Missouri, leaving all of their property behind except what could be taken in a wagon with two horses. She next moved to Commerce, Illinois, where the city of Nauvoo was later built, and a few years afterwards was again driven out by mob violence.

She immigrated to Salt Lake City in 1850 and died June 30, 1886, at Richmond, Utah. She was the mother of eight children, and at the time of her death had sixty-seven grandchildren and thirty-two great-grandchildren.

164

away our weapons. . . . Before I could get to the blacksmith's shop door to alarm the brethren, who were at prayers, the bullets were whistling amongst them. I seized my two little girls and escaped across the millpond on a slab-walk. Another sister fled with me.

A number of bullets entered my clothes, but I was not wounded. The sister, however, who was with me, cried out that she was hit. We had just reached the trunk of a fallen tree, over which I urged her, bidding her to shelter there where the bullets could not reach her, while I continued my flight to some bottom land. When the firing had ceased I went back to the scene of the massacre, for there were my husband and three sons, of whose fate I as yet knew nothing.

As I returned I found the sister in a pool of blood where she had fainted, but she was only shot through the hand. Farther on was lying dead Brother McBride, an aged white-headed revolutionary soldier. His murderer had literally cut him to pieces with an old corn-cutter. . . . Passing on I came to a scene more terrible still. . . . Emerging from the blacksmith shop was my eldest son, bearing on his shoulders his little brother Alma. "Oh! my Alma is dead!" I cried, in anguish. "No, Mother; I think Alma is not dead. But Father and brother Sardius are killed!" What an answer was this to appall me! My husband and son murdered, another little son seemingly mortally wounded, and perhaps before the dreadful night should pass the murderers would return to complete their work!

But I could not weep then. The fountain of tears was dry; the heart overburdened with its calamity, and all the mother's sense absorbed in its anxiety for the precious boy which God alone could save by his miraculous aid. The entire hip joint of my wounded boy had been shot away. Flesh, hip bone, joint, and all had been ploughed out from the muzzle of the gun which the ruffian placed to the child's hip through the logs of the shop and deliberately fired. We laid little Alma on a bed in our tent and I examined the wound. It was a ghastly sight. I knew not what to do. It was night now. There were none left from that terrible scene, throughout that long, dark night, but about half a dozen bereaved and lamenting women and the children.

Eighteen or nineteen, all grown men excepting my murdered boy and another about the same age, were dead or dying; several more of the men were wounded, hiding away, whose groans through the night too well disclosed their hiding places, while the rest of the men had fled, at the moment of the massacre, to save their lives.

The women were sobbing, in the greatest anguish of spirit; the children were crying loudly with fear and grief at the loss of fathers and brothers. . . . Yet was I there all that long, dreadful night, with my dead and my wounded, and none but God as our physician and help. "Oh, my Heavenly Father," I cried, "what shall I do? Thou seest my poor wounded boy and knowest my inexperience. Oh, Heavenly Father direct me what to do!" And then I was directed as by a voice speaking to me.

The ashes of our fire was still smouldering. We had been burning the bark of the shag-bark hickory. I was directed to take those ashes and make a lye and put a cloth saturated with it right into the wound. It hurt, but little Alma was too near dead to heed it much. Again and again I saturated the cloth and put it into the hole from which the hip joint had been ploughed, and each time mashed flesh and splinters of bone came away with the cloth, and the wound became as white as chicken's flesh. Having done as directed I again prayed to the Lord and was again instructed as distinctly as though a physician had been standing by speaking to me. Nearby was a slippery-elm tree. From this I was told to make a slippery-elm poultice and fill the wound with it. My eldest boy was sent to get the slippery-elm from the roots, the poultice was made, and the wound, which took fully a quarter of a yard of linen to cover, so large was it, was properly dressed.

It was then that I found vent to my feelings in tears and resigned myself to the anguish of the hour. And all that night we, a few poor, stricken women, were thus left there with our dead and wounded. . . .

I removed the wounded boy to a house, some distance off, the next day, and dressed his hip, the Lord directing me as before. I was reminded that in my husband's trunk there was a bottle of balsam. This I poured into the wound, greatly soothing

Alma's pain. "Alma, my child," I said, "you believe that the Lord made your hip?" "Yes, Mother." "Well, the Lord can make something there in the place of your hip, don't you believe he can, Alma?" "Do you think that the Lord can, Mother?" inquired the child, in his simplicity. "Yes, my son," I replied, "he has shown it all to me in a vision." Then I laid him comfortably on his face, and said: "Now you lie like that, and don't move, and the Lord will make you another hip."

So Alma lay on his face for five weeks, until he was entirely recovered—a flexible gristle having grown in place of the missing joint and socket, which remains to this day a marvel to physicians. On the day that he walked again I was out of the house fetching a bucket of water when I heard screams from the children. Running back, in affright, I entered, and there was Alma on the floor, dancing around, and the children screaming in astonishment and joy. It is now nearly forty years ago, but Alma has never been the least crippled during his life, and he has traveled quite a long period of the time as a missionary of the gospel and a living miracle of the power of God.

Nelson B. Lundwall, *Assorted Gems of Priceless Value* (Salt Lake City: Bookcraft, 1947), pp. 92-96.

AMANDA SMITH

"From That Moment I Had No More Fear"

All the Mormons in the neighborhood had fled out of the state, excepting a few families of the bereaved women and children who had gathered at the house of Brother David Evans, two miles from the scene of the [Haun's

Mill] massacre. To this house Alma had been carried after that fatal night. In our utter desolation, what could we women do but pray? Prayer was our only source of comfort, our Heavenly Father our only helper. None but he could save and deliver us.

One day a mobber came from the mill with the captain's fiat: "The captain says if you women don't stop your d___d praying he will send down a posse and kill every d____d one of you!" And he might as well have done it, as to stop us poor women praying in that hour of our great calamity. Our prayers were hushed in terror. We dared not let our voices be heard in the house in supplication. I could pray in my bed or in silence, but I could not live thus long. This godless silence was more intolerable than had been that night of the massacre. I could bear it no longer. I pined to hear once more my own voice in petition to my Heavenly Father. I stole down into a cornfield and crawled into a "stout of corn." It was as the temple of the Lord to me at that moment. I prayed aloud and most fervently. When I emerged from the corn a voice spoke to me. It was a voice as plain as I ever heard one. It was no silent, strong impression of the spirit, but a VOICE, repeating a verse of the Saint's hymn:

That soul who on Jesus hath leaned for repose,
I cannot, I will not desert to its foes;
That soul, though all hell should endeavor to shake,
I'll never, no never, no never forsake!

From that moment I had no more fear. . . .

Lundwall, *Assorted Gems of Priceless Value*, p. 97.

BATHSHEBA   W.   SMITH*

"The Apparently Astonished Ox"

In May 1849, about four hundred wagons were organized and started west.

In the latter part of June following, our family left our encampment. We started on our journey to the valley in a company of two hundred and eighteen wagons. These were organized into three companies, which were subdivided into companies of ten, each company properly officered. Each company also had its blacksmith and wagonmaker, equipped with proper tools for attending to their work of setting tires, shoeing animals, and repairing wagons.

Twenty-four of the wagons of our company belonged to the

*Bathsheba Wilson Smith was a charter member of the Female Relief Society organized by the Prophet Joseph Smith in Nauvoo, Illinois, on March 17, 1842, and became fourth general president of the Relief Society. She was born May 3, 1822, at Shinnston, Harrison County, West Virginia, a daughter of Mark Bigler and Susannah Ogden. In 1837 she was baptized and moved to Nauvoo, where she became acquainted with Joseph Smith's family and was married to George A. Smith, the Prophet's cousin, on July 25, 1841. They had two children. She officiated as an ordinance worker in the Nauvoo Temple, in the Endowment House in Salt Lake City, and in the Logan and Salt Lake .emples. Sister Smith was a counselor in the presidency of the central board of Relief Society from 1888 to 1892 and in the general presidency from 1892 to 1901, when she became general president. She died September 20, 1910, in Salt Lake City.

Welsh Saints, who had been led from Wales by Elder Dan Jones. They did not understand driving oxen. It was very amusing to see them yoke their cattle; two would have an animal by the horns, one by the tail, and one or two others would do their best to put on the yoke, whilst the apparently astonished ox, not at all enlightened by the gutteral sounds of the Welsh tongue, seemed perfectly at a loss what to do or to know what was wanted of him. But these Saints amply made up for their lack of skill in driving cattle by their excellent singing, which afforded us great assistance in our public meetings and helped to enliven our evenings.

On this journey my wagon was provided with projections, of about eight inches wide, on each side of the top of the box. The cover, which was high enough for us to stand erect, was widened by these projections. A frame was laid across the back part of our wagon and was corded as a bedstead; this made our sleeping very comfortable. Under our beds we stowed our heaviest articles. We had a door in one side of the wagon cover, and on the opposite side a window. A step-ladder was used to ascend to our door, which was between the wheels. . . . Our door and window could be opened and closed at pleasure. I had, hanging up on the inside, a looking-glass, candlestick, pin cushion, etc. In the center of our wagon we had room for four chairs, in which we and our two children sat and rode when we chose. The floor of our traveling house was carpeted, and we made ourselves as comfortable as we could under the circumstances.

After having experienced the common vicissitudes of that strange journey, having encountered terrible storms and endured extreme hardships, we arrived at our destination on the 5th of November, 105 days after leaving the Missouri River.

Tullidge, *The Women of Mormondom,* pp. 342-43.

Biographical Sketch

LUCY   MACK   SMITH

It was on July 8, 1776, that a daughter was born to Solomon and Lydia Mack, prosperous farming people of Gilsum, New Hampshire. Before Lucy had reached her twentieth birthday, she had met and married a young farmer from Tunbridge, Vermont, named Joseph Smith. Life began favorably for Joseph and Lucy, yet little did they dream of the strange and extraordinary events that were before them, events that were to lift their name from obscurity into undying fame. It was while renting a farm from Mrs. Smith's father, Solomon Mack, that their fourth child and third son was born; they named him Joseph Smith, Jr.

Lucy Smith and her husband became the first believers in the visions and relevations that were vouchsafed to their youthful son.

As if she had not suffered sufficiently in the loss of her husband and three grown sons in the short space of four years, Lucy Smith was called upon to part with another son, Samuel Harrison, less than five weeks after the deaths of Joseph and Hyrum. In fleeing from the mob at Carthage he had overexerted himself. In a few weeks he fell ill and died.

Her last years were spent with her family. She looked fearlessly and calmly into the future, with the firm assurance that the sacred record and the revelations given to her gifted son are God's revealed truth. She died May 5, 1855.

Mary Grant Judd, *Relief Society Magazine,* April 1943, pp. 227-31.

LUCY MACK SMITH

"Father, Mother, You Do Not Know How Happy I Am"

After attending to the usual services, namely, reading, singing, and praying, Joseph arose from his knees, and approaching Martin Harris with a solemnity that thrills through my veins to this day, when it occurs to my recollection, said, "Martin Harris, you have got to humble yourself before God this day, that you may obtain a forgiveness of your sins. If you do, it is the will of God that you should look upon the plates, in company with Oliver Cowdery and David Whitmer."

In a few minutes after this, Joseph, Martin, Oliver and David repaired to a grove, a short distance from the house, where they commenced calling upon the Lord, and continued in earnest supplication, until he permitted an angel to come down from his presence and declare to them, that all which Joseph had testified of concerning the plates was true.

When they returned to the house it was between three and four o'clock p.m. Mrs. Whitmer, Mr. Smith and myself were sitting in a bedroom at the time. On coming in, Joseph threw himself down beside me and exclaimed, "Father, Mother, you do not know how happy I am: the Lord has now caused the plates to be shown to three more besides myself. They have seen an angel, who has testified to them, and they will have to bear witness to the truth of what I have said, for now they know for themselves, that I do not go about to deceive the people, and I feel as if I was relieved of a burden which was almost too heavy for me to bear, and it rejoices my soul, that I am not any longer to be entirely alone in the world." Upon this, Martin Harris came in: he seemed almost overcome with joy, and testified boldly to what he had both seen and heard. And so did David and Oliver, adding that no tongue could express the joy of their hearts and the greatness of the things which they had both seen and heard.

Lucy Mack Smith (Preston Nibley, ed.), *History of Joseph Smith by His Mother Lucy Mack Smith* (Salt Lake City, Utah: Bookcraft, 1958), pp. 151-53.

LUCY MACK SMITH

"God Bless You, Mother!"

When they were about starting from Far West,[1] a messenger came and told us that if we ever saw our sons alive, we must go immediately to them, for they were in a wagon that would start in a few minutes for Independence, and in all probability they would never return alive. Receiving this intimation, Lucy and myself set out directly for the place. On coming within about a hundred yards of the wagon, we were compelled to stop, for we could press no further

---

[1]This event took place in Far West, Missouri, in 1838, when Joseph and Hyrum Smith had been taken prisoner.

through the crowd. I therefore appealed to those around me, exclaiming, "I am the mother of the Prophet—is there not a gentleman here, who will assist me to that wagon, that I may take a last look at my children, and speak to them once more before I die?"

Upon this, one individual volunteered to make a pathway through the army, and we passed on, threatened with death at every step, till at length we arrived at the wagon. The man who led us through the crowd spoke to Hyrum, who was sitting in front, and, telling him that his mother had come to see him, requested that he should reach his hand to me. He did so, but I was not allowed to see him; the cover was of strong cloth, and nailed down so close that he could barely get his hand through. We had merely shaken hands with him, when we were ordered away by the mob, who forbade any conversation between us, and, threatening to shoot us, they ordered the teamster to drive over us.

Our friend then conducted us to the back part of the wagon, where Joseph sat, and said, "Mr. Smith, your mother and sister are here, and wish to shake hands with you." Joseph crowded his hand through between the cover and wagon, and we caught hold of it; but he spoke not to either of us, until I said, "Joseph, do speak to your poor mother once more—I cannot bear to go till I hear your voice." "God bless you, Mother!" he sobbed out. Then a cry was raised, and the wagon dashed off, tearing him from us just as Lucy was pressing his hand to her lips, to bestow upon it a sister's last kiss—for he was then sentenced to be shot.

Smith, *History of Joseph Smith by His Mother, Lucy Mack Smith,* pp. 290-91.

" 'I Suppose,' Said I, 'You Intend to Kill Me' "

Joseph was at our house writing a letter. While he was thus engaged, I stepped to the door, and looking towards the prairie, I beheld a large company of armed men advancing towards the city, but, as I supposed it to be training day, said nothing about it.

Presently the main body came to a halt. The officers dismounting, eight of them came into the house. Thinking they had come for some refreshment, I offered them chairs, but they refused to be seated, and, placing themselves in a line across the floor, continued standing. I again requested them to sit, but they replied, "We do not choose to sit down; we have come here to kill Joe Smith and all the 'Mormons.' "

"Ah," said I, "what has Joseph Smith done, that you should want to kill him?"

"He has killed seven men in Daviess County," replied the foremost, "and we have come to kill him, and all his church."

"He has not been in Daviess County," I answered, "consequently the report must be false. Furthermore, if you should see him, you would not want to kill him."

"There is no doubt that the report is perfectly correct," rejoined the officer; "it came straight to us, and I believe it; and we were sent to kill the Prophet and all who believe in him, and I'll be d----d if I don't execute my orders."

"I suppose," said I, "you intend to kill me, with the rest?"

"Yes, we do," returned the officer.

"Very well," I continued, "I want you to act the gentleman about it, and do the job quick. Just shoot me down at once, then I shall be at rest; but I should not like to be murdered by inches."

"There it is again," said he. "You tell a 'Mormon' that you will kill him, and they will always tell you, 'That is nothing—if you kill us, we shall be happy.' "

Joseph just at this moment finished his letter, and, seeing that he was at liberty, I said, "Gentlemen, suffer me to make you acquainted with Joseph Smith, the Prophet." They stared at him as if he were a spectre. He smiled, and stepping towards them, gave each of them his hand, in a manner which convinced them that he was neither a guilty criminal nor yet a hypocrite.

Joseph then sat down and explained to them the views, feelings, etc., of the Church, and what their course had been; besides the treatment which they had received from their enemies since the first. He also argued, that if any of the brethren had broken the laws, they ought to be tried by the law, before anyone else was molested. After talking with them some time in this way, he said, "Mother, I believe I will go home now— Emma will be expecting me." At this two of the men sprang to their feet, and declared that he should not go alone, as it would be unsafe—that they would go with him, in order to protect him. Accordingly the three left together. . . .

Smith, *History of Joseph Smith by His Mother, Lucy Mack Smith*, pp. 254-56.

LUCY   MACK   SMITH

"Mark My Words"

Mr. Whitermore gave me an introduction to one Mr. Ruggles, the pastor of the Presbyterian church to which this Mr. Whitermore belonged.

"And you," said Mr. Ruggles, upon shaking hands with me, "are the mother of that poor, foolish, silly boy, Joe Smith, who pretended to translate the Book of Mormon."

I looked him steadily in the face, and replied, "I am, sir,

the mother of Joseph Smith; but why do you apply to him such epithets as those?"

"Because," said his reverence, "that he should imagine he was going to break down all other churches with that simple 'Mormon' book."

"Did you ever read that book?" I inquired.

"No," said he, "it is beneath my notice."

"But," rejoined I, "the Scriptures say, 'prove all things'; and, now, sir, let me tell you boldly, that that book contains the everlasting gospel, and it was written for the salvation of your soul, by the gift and power of the Holy Ghost."

"Pooh," said the minister, "nonsense—I am not afraid of any member of my church being led astray by such stuff; they have too much intelligence."

"Now, Mr. Ruggles," said I, and I spoke with emphasis, for the Spirit of God was upon me, "mark my words—as true as God lives, before three years we will have more than one-third of your church; and, sir, whether you believe it or not, we will take the very deacon, too."

This produced a hearty laugh at the expense of the minister.

Not to be tedious, I will say that I remained in this section of country about four weeks, during which time I labored incessantly for the truth's sake, and succeeded in gaining the hearts of many, among whom were David Dort and his wife. Many desired me to use my influence to have an elder sent into that region of country, which I agreed to do. As I was about starting home, Mr. Cooper observed that our ministers would have more influence if they dressed in broadcloth.

When I returned, I made known to Joseph the situation of things where I had been, so he despatched Brother Jared Carter to that country. And in order that he might not lack influence, he was dressed in a suit of superfine broadcloth. He went immediately into the midst of Mr. Ruggles' church, and, in a short time, brought away seventy of his best members, among whom was the deacon, just as I told the minister. This deacon was Brother Samuel Bent, who now presides over the High Council.

Smith, *History of Joseph Smith by His Mother Lucy Mack Smith*, pp. 215-17.

"Mob It Is, Then"

We proceeded on our journey, [from Palmyra to Kirtland, 1831] and arrived at Buffalo on the fifth day after leaving Waterloo.

Here we found the brethren from Colesville, who informed us that they had been detained one week at this place, waiting for the navigation to open. Also, that Mr. Smith and Hyrum had gone through to Kirtland by land, in order to be there by the first of April.

I asked them if they had confessed to the people that they were "Mormons." "No, indeed," they replied, "neither must you mention a word about your religion, for if you do you will never be able to get a house, or a boat either."

I told them I should tell the people precisely who I was; "and," continued I, "if you are ashamed of Christ, you must not expect to be prospered; and I shall wonder if we do not get to Kirtland before you."

While we were talking with the Colesville brethren, another boat landed, having on board about thirty brethren, among whom was Thomas B. Marsh, who immediately joined us, and, like the Colesville brethren, he was decidedly opposed to our attending to prayer, or making known that we were professors of religion. He said that if our company persisted in singing and praying, as we had hitherto done, we should be mobbed before the next morning.

"Mob it is, then," said I, "we shall attend to prayer before sunset, mob or no mob." Mr. Marsh, at this, left considerably irritated. I then requested brothers Humphry and Page to go around among the boatmen, and inquire for one Captain Blake, who was formerly captain of a boat belonging to my brother, General Mack, and who, upon my brother's decease, purchased the boat and still commanded the same. They went in search of the man, and soon found him, and learned from him that his boat was already laden with the usual amount of passengers and freight. He said, however, that he thought he could make room for us if we would take a deck passage. As this was our only opportunity, we moved our goods on board the next day, and by the time that we fairly settled ourselves, it began to rain. This rendered our situation very uncomfortable, and some of the sisters complained bitterly because we had not hired a house till the boat was ready to start. In fact, their case was rather a trying one, for some of them had sick children; in consequence of which, Brother Page went out for the purpose of getting a room for the women and sick children, but returned unsuccessful. At this the sisters renewed their complaints, and declared that they would have a house, let the consequences be what they might. In order to satisfy them, I set out myself, with my son William, although it was still raining very fast, to see if it were possible to procure a shelter for them and their children.

I stopped at the first tavern and inquired of the landlord if he could let me have a room for some women and children who were sick. The landlord replied that he could easily make room for them. At this, a woman who was present turned upon him very sharply, saying, "I have put up here myself, and I am not a-going to have anybody's things in my way. I'll warrant the children have got the whooping cough or measles, or some other contagious disease, and, if they come, I will go somewhere else."

"Why, madam," said the landlord, "that is not necessary, you can still have one large room."

"I don't care," said she, "I want 'em both, and if I can't have 'em, I won't stay—that's it."

"Never mind," said I, "it is no matter; I suppose I can get a room somewhere else, just as well."

"No, you can't though," rejoined the lady, "for we hunted all over the town and we could not find one single one till we got here."

I left immediately and went on my way. Presently I came to a long row of rooms, one of which appeared to be almost vacant. I inquired if it could be rented for a few days. The owner of the buildings I found to be a cheerful old lady, near seventy years of age. I mentioned the circumstances to her, as I before had done to the landlord.

"Well, I don't know," said she; "where be you going?"

"To Kirtland," I replied.

"What be you?" said she. "Be you Baptists?"

I told her that we were "Mormons."

"Mormons!" ejaculated she, in a quick, good-natured tone. "What be they? I never heard of them before."

"I told you that we were 'Mormons,' " I replied, "because that is what the world calls us, but the only name we acknowledge is Latter-day Saints."

"Latter-day Saints!" rejoined she. "I never heard of them either."

I then informed her that this church was brought forth through the instrumentality of a prophet, and that I was the mother of this prophet.

"What!" said she, a "prophet in these days! I never heard of the like in my life; and if you will come and sit with me, you shall have a room for your sisters and their children, but you yourself must come and stay with me, and tell me about it."

Smith, *History of Joseph Smith by His Mother Lucy Mack Smith*, pp. 198-202.

LUCY   MACK   SMITH

"Is the Book of Mormon True?"

A man on shore cried, "Is the Book of Mormon true?" [Lucy was on a boat on the Erie Canal in Buffalo, New York.]

"That book," replied I, "was brought forth by the power of God, and translated by the gift of the Holy Ghost; and, if I could make my voice sound as loud as the trumpet of Michael, the Archangel, I would declare the truth from land to land, and from sea to sea, and the echo should reach to every isle, until every member of the family of Adam should be left without excuse. For I do testify that God has revealed himself to man again in these last days, and set his hand to gather his people upon a goodly land, and, if they obey his commandments, it shall be unto them for an inheritance; whereas, if they rebel against his law, his hand will be against them to scatter them abroad, and cut them off from the face of the earth; and that he has commenced a work which will prove a savor of life unto life, or of death unto death, to every one that stands here this day—of life unto life—if you will receive it, or of death unto death, if you reject the counsel of God, for every man shall have the desires of his heart; if he desires the truth, he may hear and live, but if he tramples upon the simplicity of the word of God, he will shut the gate of heaven against himself."

Smith, *History of Joseph Smith by His Mother Lucy Mack Smith*, p. 204.

LUCY   MACK   SMITH

"I Called Upon the Elders"

I now concluded to devote the most of my time to the study of the Bible, Book of Mormon, and Doctrine and Covenants, but a circumstance occurred which deprived me of the privilege. One day upon going down stairs to dinner, I incautiously set my foot upon a round stick, that lay near the top of the stairs. This, rolling under my foot, pitched me forward down the steps; my head was severely bruised in falling; however, I said but little about it, thinking I should be better soon.

In the afternoon, I went with my husband to a blessing meeting; I took cold, and an inflammation settled in my eyes, which increased until I became entirely blind. The distress which I suffered for a few days surpasses all description. Every effort was made by my friends to relieve me, but all in vain. I called upon the elders, and requested them to pray to the Lord, that I might be able to see, so as to be able to read without even wearing spectacles. They did so, and when they took their hands off my head, I read two lines in the Book of Mormon; and although I am now seventy years old, I have never worn glasses since.

Smith, *History of Joseph Smith by His Mother Lucy Mack Smith*, pp. 237-38.

LUCY MACK SMITH

"Mother, Weep Not for Us"

Mother Smith, as she was called, accepted the mission of her son, the Prophet Joseph, from the first. . . .

At the death of her husband, Lucy writes: "I then thought that the greatest grief which was possible for me to feel had fallen upon me in the death of my beloved husband—but when I entered the room, and saw my murdered sons extended both at once before my eyes, and heard the sobs and groans of my family, and the cries of 'Father! Husband! Brothers!' from the lips of their wives, children, brothers, and sisters, it was too much. I sank back crying to the Lord in the agony of my soul, 'My God, my God, why hast thou forsaken this family!' A voice replied, 'I have taken them to myself, that they might have rest.' As for myself, I was swallowed up in the depths of my afflictions. . . . at that moment how my mind flew through every scene of sorrow and distress which we had passed together, in which they had shown the innocence and sympathy which filled their guileless hearts. As I looked upon their peaceful countenances, I seemed almost to hear them say, 'Mother, weep not for us, we have overcome the world by love; we carried to them the gospel, that their souls might be saved; they slew us for our testimony, and thus placed us beyond their power; their ascendency is for a moment, ours is an eternal triumph.' "

Relief Society Magazine, May 1942, pp. 295-96.

MARY   BAILEY   SMITH*

"They Burned the House Down to the Ground"

The day had finally arrived, for which Samuel and Mary had been planning all summer, and "there was born unto Samuel a son, whom he called by his own name." But when Samuel heard rumors of trouble from the mobs, his rejoicing soon gave way to fear for the safety of his loved ones. If he had a "means of conveyance," he could move his family to Far West, where they would be safe with his mother. So, reluctantly leaving Mary for a short time, he went to Far West for a team and wagon.

But Mary was no sooner left alone, than the mob appeared. Many years later, Mary's second daughter told the story of what happened that day:

"When my brother was three days old, my mother was taken from the house. They took her by picking up the featherbed, and

*Mary Bailey Smith was reared in New England; her father was Joshua Bailey. Baptized on June 26, 1832, she then traveled to Kirtland, Ohio, to be with the Saints. She was married to Samuel Smith, a brother of the Prophet Joseph Smith, on August 13, 1834; they had four children. She died giving birth to her third daughter; the baby died shortly after she did.

carried her, with her babe, out into the sleet and rain, and placed the bed on the ground. Then they placed the other two children, my sister Susan and myself, on the bed with her. Then, giving her a few necessary things she asked for, they burned the house down to the ground.

"With her frightened children cuddled close, Mary prayed desperately for deliverance from her helpless plight, while anguished thoughts—such as these—raced through her mind: 'Why, oh why, must I go through this ordeal alone? Samuel would have known what to do. How can I let them burn our little home, and everything we own—our food—our clothes—all the things Samuel made for me—everything I found so much joy in making for him and the children—the treasures we brought from Kirtland—even my keepsakes from New England! We put so much of our hopes and dreams for the future into that home! And now they are burning it! Why, oh, why!

" 'Dear God, you have always heard my prayers before! Why am I forsaken now—to suffer this alone! Please remember all your promises to Samuel and me, and give me enough faith to claim their fulfillment.

" 'Help me to be brave, dear Father, for the sake of my precious children. Please save the life of my newborn son; and keep our children safe—for Samuel. And let me live to take care of them for him! Dear Lord, please send someone to help us!' "

Mother Smith tells the rest of the story:

"One of the neighbors offered to furnish a team and a small boy to drive it, if she would start immediately. To this she agreed. A lumber wagon was brought, and she, with her bed, her children, and very little clothing, either for them or herself, was put upon it and sent to Far West, under the care of a boy eleven years of age.

"The following day, Samuel started home from Far West, although the rain was falling fast and had been all the night previous. He had proceeded ten miles, when he met his wife and children, exposed to the inclemency of the weather, and dripping with wet. He returned with them to Far West, where they arrived thirty-six hours after they left Marrowbone, without having taken any nourishment from the time they left home!

"Mary was entirely speechless and stiff with the cold. We laid her on a bed, and my husband and sons administered to her by the laying on of hands. Then we changed her clothing and put her into warm blankets. She opened her eyes and seemed to revive a little. I continued to employ every means that lay in my power for her recovery, and in this I was much assisted by Emma [Smith] and my daughters."

Ruby K. Smith, *Mary Bailey* (Salt Lake City: Deseret Book Co., 1954), pp. 70-71.

Biographical Sketch

MARY FIELDING SMITH

Mary Fielding Smith was born July 21, 1801, in Honidon, Bedfordshire, England, a daughter of John Fielding and Rachel Ibbolson.

In 1832 Mary's brother, Joseph, and her sister, Mercy, emigrated to Toronto, Canada. Mary followed in 1834. The three Fieldings were baptized by Parley P. Pratt in May 1836; John Taylor, their close friend, was also converted at the same time. In the spring of 1837 the Fieldings moved to Kirtland, Ohio.

Mary, a well-educated, refined, beautiful woman, married Hyrum Smith December 24, 1837, at age thirty-six; Hyrum was one year older. Hyrum's first wife, Jerusha, had died, leaving him with five small children.

Mary Fielding Smith was blessed with two children. The eldest was Joseph F. Smith, who became the sixth president of the Church; he was born in Far West, Missouri, on November 13, 1838. Her second child was Martha Ann, born May 14, 1841, in Nauvoo, Illinois.

Mary Fielding Smith emigrated to the West in 1848. She died in Salt Lake City September 21, 1852. She has numerous faithful descendants and is honored as one of the most noble women of this dispensation. The following was written of her at the time of her death:

"The deceased was truly a 'mother in Israel,' and her name and deeds will be had in everlasting remembrance, associated as they are, with the persecutions of the Saints, and those tragic scenes that can never be forgotten. Possessed, in a superlative degree, of those peculiar qualifications that support and invigorate the mind in adversity, she endured afflictions and overcame difficulties with a degree of patience and perseverance worthy of imitation."[1]

---

[1]Joseph Fielding Smith, *Life of Joseph F. Smith* (Salt Lake City: Deseret News Press, 1938), p. 161.

MARY   FIELDING   SMITH

"Breathe More Softly"

I felt much pleased to see Sister Walton and Snider who arrived here [Kirtland, Ohio] on Saturday about noon, having left Brother Joseph Smith and Brigham [Young] about twenty miles from Fairport to evade the mobbers. They were to come home in Dr. Avard's carriage, and expected to arrive about 10 o'clock at night, but to their great disappointment they were prevented in a most grievous manner.

They had got within four miles of home, after a very fatiguing journey, much pleased with their visit to Canada and greatly anticipating the pleasure of seeing their homes and families, when they were surrounded with a mob and taken back to Painesville and secured, as was supposed, in a tavern where they intended to hold a mock trial, but to the disappointment of the wretches, the housekeeper was a member of the Church, who assisted our beloved brethren in making their escape, but as "Brother Joseph" says, not by a basket let down through the window, but by the kitchen door.

No doubt the hand of the Lord was in it, or it could not have been effected. The day had been extremely wet and the night was unusually dark and you may try if you can to conceive what the situation was. They hardly knew which way to start as it had by that time got to be about ten o'clock. The first step they took was to find the woods as quickly as possible where they thought they should be safe, but in order to reach there, they had to lie down in a swamp by an old log, just where they happened to be. So determinedly were they pursued by their mad enemies in every direction, and sometimes so closely, that "Brother Joseph" was obliged to entreat "Brother Brigham" to breathe more softly if he meant to escape. When they would run or walk they took each other by the hand and covenanted to live and die together.

Owing to the darkness of the night, their pursuers had to carry lighted torches, which was one means of the escape of our beloved sufferers, as they could see them in every direction while they were climbing over fences or traveling through bush or cane fields, until about 12 o'clock. After traveling on foot along muddy, slippery roads until near three in the morning, they arrived safely home before sunrise, and thank God it was so.

Notwithstanding all that he had to endure, he appeared in the House of the Lord throughout the Sabbath, in excellent spirit, spoke in a very powerful manner, and blessed the congregation in the name of the Lord; and I do assure you the Saints felt the blessings upon him. Brother Rigdon, through his great weariness, and a small hurt, received from a fall, did not attend the House, but is now well. I suppose all these things will only add another gem to their crown.

Don C. Corbett, *Mary Fielding Smith, Daughter of Britain* (Salt Lake City: Deseret Book Co., 1966), pp. 38-39.

"The Lord Knows What Is Best for Us"

As it respects myself, it is now so long since I wrote to you,[1] and so many important things have transpired, and so great have been my afflictions, etc., that I know not where to begin; but I can say, hitherto has the Lord preserved me, and I am still among the living to praise him, as I do today. I have, to be sure, been called to drink of the bitter cup; but you know, my beloved brother, this makes the sweet sweeter.

You have, I suppose, heard of the imprisonment of my dear husband, with his brother, Joseph, Elder Rigdon, and others, who were kept from us nearly six months; and I suppose no one felt the painful effects of their confinement more than myself. I was left in a way that called for the exercise of all the courage and grace I possessed. My husband was taken from me by an armed force, at a time when I needed, in a particular manner, the kindest care and attention of such a friend, instead of which, the care of a large family was suddenly and unexpectedly left upon myself, and, in a few days after, my dear little Joseph F. was added to the number. Shortly after his birth I took a severe cold, which brought on chills and fevers; this, together with the anxiety of mind I had to endure, threatened to bring me to the gates of death. I was at least four months entirely unable to take any care either of myself or child; but the Lord was merciful in ordering things that my dear sister could be with me. Her child was five months old when mine was born, so she had strength given her to nurse them both.

You will also have heard of our being driven as a people, from the States, and from our homes; this happened during my sickness, and I had to be removed more than two hundred miles, chiefly on my bed. I suffered much on my journey; but in three

---

[1]Her brother, Joseph Fielding, who was on a mission in England.

or four weeks after we arrived in Illinois, I began to mend, and my health is now as good as ever. It is now little more than a month since the Lord, in his marvelous power, returned my dear husband, with the rest of the brethren, to their families, in tolerable health. We are now living in Commerce, on the bank of the great Mississippi River. The situation is very pleasant; you would be much pleased to see it. How long we may be permitted to enjoy it I know not; but the Lord knows what is best for us. I feel but little concern about where I am, if I can keep my mind staid upon God; for, you know in this there is perfect peace. I believe the Lord is overruling all things for our good. I suppose our enemies look upon us with astonishment and disappointment. . . .

O, my dear brother, I must tell you, for your comfort, that my hope is full, and it is a glorious hope; and though I have been left for near six months in widowhood, in the time of great affliction, and was called to take joyfully or otherwise, the spoiling of almost all our goods, in the absence of my husband, and all unlawfully, just for the gospel's sake (for the judge himself declared that he was kept in prison for no other reason than because he was a friend to his brother), yet I do not feel in the least discouraged; now though my sister and I are here together in a strange land, we have been enabled to rejoice, in the midst of our privations and persecutions, that we were counted worthy to suffer these things, so that we may, with the ancient saints who suffered in like manner, inherit the same glorious reward. If it had not been for this hope, I should have sunk before this; but, blessed be the God and rock of my salvation, here I am, and am perfectly satisfied and happy, having not the smallest desire to go one step backward. . . .

The more I see of the dealing of our Heavenly Father with us as a people, the more I am constrained to rejoice that I was ever made acquainted with the everlasting covenant. O may the Lord keep me faithful.

Corbett, *Mary Fielding Smith, Daughter of Britain,* pp. 99-100.

"Well, Mary, the Cattle Are Gone"

As told by Joseph F. Smith

We camped one evening in an open prairie on the Missouri River bottoms, by the side of a small spring creek which emptied into the river about three quarters of a mile from us. We were in plain sight of the river and could apparently see over every foot of the little open prairie where we were camped, to the river on the southwest, to the bluffs on the northwest, and to the timber which skirted the prairie on the right and left. Camping nearby, on the other side of the creek, were some men with a herd of beef cattle. . . .

We usually unyoked our oxen and turned them loose to feed during our encampments at night, but this time, on account of the proximity of this herd of cattle, fearing that they might get mixed up and driven off with them, we turned our oxen out to feed in their yokes. Next morning when we came to look them up, to our great disappointment our best yoke of oxen was not to be found. Uncle [Joseph] Fielding and I spent all the morning, well nigh until noon, hunting for them, but to no avail. The grass was tall, and in the morning was wet with heavy dew. Tramping through this grass and through the woods and over the bluff, we were soaked to the skin, fatigued, disheartened, and almost exhausted.

In this pitiable plight I was the first to return to our wagons, and as I approached I saw my mother kneeling down to prayer. I halted for a moment and then drew gently near enough to hear her pleading with the Lord not to suffer us to be left in this helpless condition, but to lead us to recover our lost team, that we might continue our travels in safety. When she arose from her knees I was standing nearby. The first expression I caught upon her precious face was a lovely smile which, discouraged as I was, gave me renewed hope and an assurance I had not felt before. A few moments later Uncle Joseph Fielding came to the camp, wet with the dews, faint, fatigued, and thoroughly disheartened. His first words were: "Well, Mary, the cattle are gone!"

Mother replied in a voice which fairly rang with cheerfulness, "Never mind; your breakfast has been waiting for hours, and now, while you and Joseph are eating, I will just take a walk out and see if I can find the cattle."

My uncle held up his hands in blank astonishment, and if the Missouri River had suddenly turned to run upstream, neither of us could have been much more surprised. "Why, Mary," he exclaimed, "what do you mean? We have been all over this country, all through the timber and through the herd of cattle, and our oxen are gone—they are not to be found. I believe they have been driven off, and it is useless for you to attempt to do such a thing as to hunt for them."

"Never mind me," said Mother; "get your breakfast and I will see," and she started towards the river, following down spring creek. Before she was out of speaking distance the man in charge of the herd of beef cattle rode up from the opposite side of the creek and called out: "Madam, I saw your oxen over in that direction about daybreak," pointing in the opposite direction from that in which Mother was going. We heard plainly what he said, but Mother went right on and did not even turn her head to look at him. A moment later the man rode off rapidly toward his herd, which had been gathered in the opening near the edge of the woods, and they were soon under full drive for the road leading toward Savannah and soon disappeared from view.

My mother continued straight down the little stream of water until she stood almost on the bank of the river. And then she beckoned to us. I was watching her every movement and was determined that she should not get out of my sight. Instantly we rose from the "mess-chest" on which our breakfast had been spread and started toward her. And like John, who outran the other disciple to the sepulchre, I outran my uncle and came first to the spot where my mother stood. There I saw our oxen fastened to a clump of willows growing in the bottom of a deep gulch which had been washed out of the sandy bank of the river by the little spring creek, perfectly concealed from view. We were not long in releasing them from bondage and getting back to our camp, where the other cattle had been fastened to the wagon wheels all the morning. And we were soon on our way home rejoicing.

Smith, *Life of Joseph F. Smith*, pp. 131-33.

MARY   FIELDING   SMITH

"I See No Necessity for Us to Wait for Them"

As told by Joseph F. Smith

Early next morning, the captain gave notice to the company to arise, hitch up, and roll over the mountain into the valley.

To our consternation when we gathered up, our cattle, the essential part of our means of transportation, for some reason had strayed away and were not to be found with the herd. A brother of mine (John) who was also a . . . scout at that time, then obtained a horse and rode back over the road in search of the lost cattle. The captain ordered the march to begin, and, regardless of our predicament, the company started out, up the mountain. The morning sun was then shining brightly, without a cloud appearing anywhere in the sky. I had happened to hear the promise of my dear mother that we would beat the captain into the valley, and would not ask any help from him either.

I sat in the front of the wagon with the team we had in hand hitched to the wheels, while my brother was absent hunting the others. I saw the company wending its slow way up the hill, the animals struggling to pull their heavy loads. The forward teams now had almost reached the summit of the hill, and I said to myself, "True enough, we have come thus far, and we have been blessed, and not the slightest help from anyone has been asked by us." But the last promise seemed to be now impossible; the last hope of getting into the valley before the rest of our company was vanishing, in my opinion.

You have doubtless heard descriptions of the terrible thunderstorms that sometimes visit the mountains. The pure, crystal streams a few moments before flow gently down their channels; but after one of these rains, in a few minutes they become raging torrents, muddy and sometimes bringing down fallen trees and roots and rocks. All of a sudden, and in less time than I am taking to tell you, a big, dark, heavy cloud rose from the northwest, going directly southeast. In a few minutes it burst in such terrific fury that the cattle could not face the storm, and the captain seemed forced to direct the company to unhitch the teams, turn them loose, and block the wheels to keep the wagons from running down the hill. The cattle fled before the storm down into the entrance into Parley's Canyon, from the park, into and through the brush.

Luckily, the storm lasted only a short time. As it ceased to rain, and the wind ceased to blow, my brother John drove up with our cattle. We then hitched them to the wagon, and the question was asked by my uncle of Mother: "Mary, what shall we do? Go on, or wait for the company to gather up their teams?" She said: "Joseph [that was her brother's name], they have not waited for us, and I see no necessity for us to wait for them."

So we hitched up and rolled up the mountain, leaving the company behind, and this was on the 23rd day of September, 1848. We reached the old Fort about 10 o'clock that night. The next morning, in the Old Bowery, we had the privilege of listening to President Brigham Young and President Kimball, Erastus Snow, and some others, give some very excellent instructions. Then, on the afternoon of that Sunday, we went out and met our friends coming in, very dusty, and very footsore, and very tired.

Smith, *Life of Joseph F. Smith*, pp. 154-155.

"*Widow Smith, It's a Shame That You Should Have to Pay Tithing*"

As told by Joseph F. Smith

I recollect very vividly a circumstance that occurred in the days of my childhood. My mother was a widow with a large family to provide for. One spring when we opened our potato pits she had her boys get a load of the best potatoes, and she took them to the tithing office; potatoes were scarce that season. I was a little boy at the time and drove the team. When we drove up to the steps of the tithing office, ready to unload the potatoes, one of the clerks came out and said to my mother: "Widow Smith, it's a shame that you should have to pay tithing."

He said a number of other things that I remember well, but they are not necessary for me to repeat here. The first two letters of the name of that tithing clerk were William Thompson, and he chided my mother for paying her tithing, called her anything but wise and prudent, and said there were others able to work that were supported from the tithing office.

My mother turned upon him and said: "William, you ought to be ashamed of yourself. Would you deny me a blessing? If I did not pay my tithing I should expect the Lord to withhold his blessings from me. I pay my tithing, not only because it is a law of God but because I expect a blessing by doing it. By keeping this and other laws, I expect to prosper and to be able to provide for my family."

Though she was a widow, you may turn to the records of the Church from the beginning unto the day of her death, and you will find that she never received a farthing from the Church to help her support herself and her family. But she paid in thousands of dollars in wheat, potatoes, corn, vegetables, meat, etc. The tithes of her sheep and cattle, the tenth pound of her butter, her tenth chicken, the tenth of her eggs, the tenth pig, the tenth calf, the tenth colt, a tenth of everything she raised was paid. Here sits my brother, who can bear testimony to the truth of what I say, as can others who knew her. She prospered because she obeyed the laws of God. She had abundance to sustain her family. We never lacked so much as many others did; for while we found nettle greens most acceptable when we first came to the valley, and while we enjoyed thistle roots, segoes, and all that kind of thing, we were no worse off than thousands of others, and not so bad off as many, for we were never without cornmeal and milk and butter, to my knowledge. Then that widow had her name recorded in the book of the law of the Lord. That widow was entitled to the privileges of the House of God. No ordinance of the gospel could be denied her, for she was obedient to the laws of God. . . .

Smith, *Life of Joseph F. Smith*, pp. 158-60.

MARY FIELDING SMITH

"I Could Have Endured a Hundred Lashes"

As told by Joseph F. Smith

When I was a child, somewhat a wayward, disobedient little boy—not that I was wilfully disobedient, but I would forget what I ought to do—I would go off with playful boys and be absent when I should have been at home, and I would forget to do things I was asked to do. Then I would go home, feel guilty, know that I was guilty, that I had neglected my duty, and that I deserved punishment.

On one occasion I had done something that was not just right, and my mother said to me, "Now, Joseph, if you do that again I shall have to whip you." Well, time went on, and by and by, I forgot it, and I did something similar again. The one thing that I admired more, perhaps, than any secondary thing in her was that when she made a promise she kept it. She never made a promise, that I know of, that she did not keep.

Well, I was called to account. She said, "Now, I told you. You knew that if you did this I would have to whip you, for I said I would. I must do it. I do not want to do it. It hurts me worse than it does you, but I must whip you."

Well, she had a little rawhide, already there, and while she was talking, or reasoning with me, showing me how much I deserved it and how painful it was to her to inflict the punishment I deserved, I had only one thought and that was: "For goodness sake, whip me; do not reason with me," for I felt the lash of her just criticism and admonition a thousandfold worse than I did the switch. I felt as if, when she laid the lash on me, I had at least partly paid my debt and had answered for my wrong doing. Her reasoning cut me down into the quick; it made me feel sorry to the very core.

I could have endured a hundred lashes with the rawhide better than I could endure a ten-minutes' talk in which I felt and was made to feel that the punishment inflicted upon me was painful to her that I loved—punishment upon my mother!

Joseph F. Smith, *Gospel Doctrine* (Salt Lake City: Deseret Book Co., 1939), pp. 317-18.

"*The Love of a True Mother*"

As told by Joseph F. Smith

I learned in my childhood, as most children probably have learned, more or less at least, that no love in all the world can equal the love of a true mother.

I did not think in those days, and still I am at a loss to know, how it would be possible for anyone to love her children more truly than did my mother. I have felt sometimes, how could even the Father love his children more than my mother loved her children? It was life to me; it was strength; it was encouragement; it was love that begat love or liking in myself. I knew she loved me with all her heart. She loved her children with all her soul. She would toil and labor and sacrifice herself, day and night, for the temporal comforts and blessings that she could meagerly give, through the results of her own labors, to her children. There was no sacrifice of self—of her own time, of her leisure or pleasure, or opportunities for rest—that was considered for a moment, when it was compared with her duty and her love for her children.

When I was fifteen years of age and called to go to a foreign country to preach the gospel—or to learn how and to learn it for myself—the strongest anchor that was fixed in my life and that helped to hold my ambition and my desire steady, to bring me upon a level and keep me straight, was that love that I knew she who bore me into the world had for me.

Only a little boy, not matured at all in judgment, without the advantage of education, I was thrown in the midst of the greatest allurements and temptations that it was possible for any boy or any man to be subjected to and yet, whenever these temptations became most alluring and most tempting to me, the first thought that arose in my soul was this: Remember the love of your mother. Remember how she strove for your welfare. Remember how willing she was to sacrifice her life for your good. Remember what she taught you in your childhood and how she insisted upon your reading the New Testament—the only book, except a few little school books, that we had in the family or that was within reach of us at that time. This feeling toward my mother became a defense, a barrier between me and temptation, so that I could turn aside from temptation and sin, by the help of the Lord and the love begotten in my soul, toward her who I knew loved me more than anybody else in all the world and more than any other living being could love me.

A wife may love her husband, but it is different to that of the love of mother to her child. The true mother, the mother who has the fear of God and the love of truth in her soul, would never hide from danger or evil and leave her child exposed to it. But as natural as it is for the sparks to fly upward, as natural as it is to breathe the breath of life, if there were danger coming to her child, she would step between the child and that danger; she would defend her child to the uttermost. Her life would be nothing in the balance in comparison with the life of her child. That is the love of true motherhood for children.

Her love for her husband would be different, for if danger should come to him, as natural as it would be for her to step between her child and danger, instead, her disposition would be to step behind her husband for protection, and that is the difference between the love of mother for children and the love of wife for husband—there is a great difference between the two.

Smith, *Gospel Doctrine*, pp. 314-15.

SARAH   FARR   SMITH*

"A Pioneer Mother"

President Smith often spoke of his
boyhood days and of his mother. Let us read his words:

"I am standing here today (in the Tabernacle) not more
than about three hundred yards from the very spot where I first
breathed the breath of life. It was just across the street (from
the Tabernacle) in a little humble home, an adobe house with
four or five rooms, surrounded by a little garden and orchard.
That is where I began. Salt Lake City at that time was a village. We did not have any water pipes. All our water was picked
up in buckets and barrels at the side of the ditches that ran down
our streets, and then it was carried to the house in smaller re-
ceptacles. We did not have any electric lights in those days. We
had tallow candles, or kerosene oil lamps, but no electric lights.
The gas did come a little later while I was a child. . . .

"I was trained at the knee of a Latter-day Saint mother.
One of the first things I remember was when she took me by the

*Sarah Farr Smith was born in Salt Lake City on October 30, 1849, a daughter
of Lorin Farr and Nancy Chase. She was married to John Henry Smith on October 20,
1866. One of her children, George Albert Smith, became the eighth president of the
Church. She died in February 1921.

hand and led me upstairs. In the room there were two beds, the bed in which my parents slept and a little trundle bed over on the other side. I can remember it as if it were yesterday. When we got upstairs, she sat down by my little trundle bed. She had me kneel in front of her. She folded my hands and took them in hers, and taught me my first prayer. I will never forget it. I do not want to forget it. It is one of the loveliest memories that I have in life, an angelic mother sitting down by my bedside and teaching me to pray.

"It was such a simple prayer but I can repeat it today.

" 'Now I lay me down to sleep. I pray the Lord my soul to keep. If I should die before I wake, I pray the Lord my soul to take.'

"That was my first prayer. That prayer opened for me the windows to heaven. That prayer extended to me the hand of my Father in heaven, for she had explained to me what it meant as far as a little child could understand.

". . . As long as she lived upon the earth, I was taught to love my Heavenly Father. I had an angel mother, for she was an angel. . . ."

Children's Friend, May 1947, p. 190.

SARAH FARR SMITH

"She Was Unusually Anxious About Me"

As told by George Albert Smith

When I was a child I became very ill. The doctor said I had typhoid fever and should be in bed for at least three weeks. He told Mother to give me no solid food but to have me drink some coffee.

When he went away, I told Mother that I didn't want any coffee. I had been taught that the Word of Wisdom, given by the Lord to Joseph Smith, advised us not to use coffee.

Mother had brought three children into the world, and two had died. She was unusually anxious about me.

I asked her to send for Brother Hawks, one of our ward teachers. He was a worker at the foundry, and a poor and humble man of great faith in the power of the Lord. He came, administered to me, and blessed me that I might be healed.

When the doctor came the next morning I was playing outside with the other children. He was surprised. He examined me and discovered that my fever was gone and that I seemed to be well.

I was grateful to the Lord for my recovery. I was sure that he had healed me.

Hartshorn, *Memories of Mothers*, p. 29.

Biographical Sketch

ELIZA R. SNOW

Eliza Roxey Snow—secretary of the first Relief Society, organized by the Prophet Joseph Smith in Nauvoo, Illinois, March 17, 1842, and second general president of the Relief Society (1866-87)—was born January 21, 1804, at Becket, Berkshire County, Massachusetts, a daughter of Oliver Snow and Rosetta Leonora Pettibone. She was baptized April 5, 1835, in Mantua, Ohio, and emigrated to Utah in September 1847.

A brilliant, versatile, and highly spiritual woman, Eliza R. Snow was a student of literature and a poet as well as an executive and organizer of rare ability. At the age of 22 she wrote for the press a requiem for John Adams and Thomas Jefferson. Her first prize story was published in Godey's *Lady's Magazine*. She was also the author of a book of poems and of a number of hymns, including "O My Father."

In 1854 she commenced organizing ward Relief Societies and acted as president of all the women's organizations in the Church until 1880, when President John Taylor separated the different organizations and set her apart as president of the Relief Society.

When the Endowment House in Salt Lake City was dedicated in 1855, Eliza was called by President Brigham Young to preside over the women's department. She was also president of the Deseret Hospital board and was a member of the Polysophical Society founded in 1854 by Lorenzo Snow, her brother, and William Eddington. She went to Palestine in 1872 with the George A. Smith company of missionaries; they returned in 1873. Sister Snow died in Salt Lake City on December 5, 1887.

Jenson, *LDS Biographical Encyclopedia*, vol. 4, p. 197.

ELIZA   R.   SNOW

"All Were Cheerful"

We were two days on our way to Far West and stopped overnight at what was called the Half-way House, a log building perhaps twenty feet square, with the chinkings between the logs, minus—they probably having been burned for firewood—the owner of the house, Brother Littlefield, having left with his family to escape being robbed; and the north wind had free ingress through the openings wide enough for cats to crawl through. This had been the lodging place of the hundreds who had preceded us, and on the present occasion proved the almost shelterless shelter of seventy-five or eighty souls. To say lodging would be a hoax, although places were allotted to a few aged and feeble, to lie down, while the rest of us either sat or stood or both, all night. My sister and I managed so that Mother lay down, and we sat by (on the floor, of course), to prevent her being trampled on, for the crowd was such that people were hardly responsible for their movements.

It was past the middle of December, and the cold was so intense that, in spite of well packing, our food was frozen, hard, bread and all, and although a blazing fire was burning on one side of the room, we could not get to it to thaw our suppers, and had to resort to the next expediency, which was this: The boys milked, and while one strained the milk, another held the pan (for there was no chance for putting anything down); then, while one held a bowl of warm milk, another would, as expeditiously as possible, thinly slice the frozen bread into it, and thus we managed for supper. In the morning, we were less crowded, as some started very early, and we toasted our bread and thawed our meat before the fire. But, withal, that was a very merry night. None but saints can be happy under every circumstance. About twenty feet from the house was a shed, in the center of which the brethren built a roaring fire, around which some of them stood and sang songs and hymns all night, while others parched corn and roasted frosted potatoes, etc. Not a complaint was heard—all were cheerful, and, judging from appearances, strangers would have taken us to be pleasure excursionists rather than a band of gubernatorial exiles.

Tullidge, *The Women of Mormondom,* pp. 145-46.

ELIZA R. SNOW

"I Think This Will Cure You of Your Faith"

The clemency of our law-abiding, citizen-expelling Governor [Lilburn W. Boggs of Missouri] allowed us ten days to leave our county, and, till the expiration of that term, a posse of militia was to guard us against mobs; but it would be very difficult to tell which was better, the militia or the mob—nothing was too mean for the militia to perform —no property was safe within the reach of those men.

One morning, while we were hard at work, preparing for our exit, the former occupant of our house entered, and in an impudent and arrogant manner inquired how soon we should be out of it. My American blood warmed to the temperature of an insulted, free-born citizen, as I looked at him and thought, poor man, you little think with whom you have to deal—God lives! He certainly overruled in that instance, for those wicked men never got possession of that property, although my father sacrificed it to American mobocracy.

In assisting widows and others who required help, my father's time was so occupied that we did not start until the morning of the 10th, the last day of the allotted grace. The weather was very cold and the ground covered with snow. After assisting in the arrangements for the journey, and shivering with cold, in order to warm my aching feet, I walked until the teams overtook me. In the meantime, I met one of the so-called militia, who accosted me with, "Well, I think this will cure you of your faith!" Looking him steadily in the eye, I replied, "No, sir; it will take more than *this* to cure me of my faith." His countenance suddenly fell, and he responded, "I must confess, you are a better soldier than I am." I passed on, thinking that, unless he was above the average of his fellows in that section, I was not highly complimented by his confession. It is true our hardships and privations were sufficient to have disheartened any but the Saints of the living God—those who were prompted by higher than earthly motives, and trusting in the arm of Jehovah.

Tullidge, *The Women of Mormondom*, pp. 143-45.

"Kind Sisters Stood Holding Dishes to Catch the Water"

I was informed that on the first night of the encampment nine children were born into the world, and from that time, as we journeyed onward [from Nauvoo westward in 1846], mothers gave birth to offspring under almost every variety of circumstances imaginable, except those to which they had been accustomed; some in tents, others in wagons—in rainstorms and in snowstorms. I heard of one birth which occurred under the rude shelter of a hut, the sides of which were formed of blankets fastened to poles stuck in the ground, with a bark roof through which the rain was dripping. Kind sisters stood holding dishes to catch the water as it fell, thus protecting the newcomer and its mother from a shower-bath as the little innocent first entered on the stage of human life; and through faith in the great ruler of events, no harm resulted to either.

Let it be remembered that the mothers of these wilderness-born babes were not savages, accustomed to roam the forest and brave the storm and tempest—those who had never known the comforts and delicacies of civilization and refinement. They were not those who, in the wilds of nature, nursed their offspring amid reeds and rushes, or in the recesses of rocky caverns; most of them were born and educated in the eastern states—had there embraced the gospel as taught by Jesus and his apostles, and, for the sake of their religion, had gathered with the Saints, and under trying circumstances had assisted, by their faith, patience, and energies, in making Nauvoo what its name indicates, "the beautiful." There they had lovely homes, decorated with flowers and enriched with choice fruit trees, just beginning to yield plentifully.

To these homes, without lease or sale, they had just bade a final adieu, and with what little of their substance could be packed into one, two, and in some instances, three wagons, had started out, desertward, for—where? To this question the only response at that time was, God knows.

Tullidge, *The Women of Mormondom*, pp. 307-308.

E L I Z A   R .   S N O W

"Sisters Walked All Day, Rain or Shine"

Brother Markham exchanged our buggy or a lumber wagon,[1] and in performing an act of generosity to others, so filled it as to give Sister M. and me barely room to sit in front. And when we started again, Sister M. and I were seated on a chest with brass-kettle and soapbox for our footstools, and were happy in being as comfortably situated as we were; and well we might be, for many of our sisters walked all day, rain or shine, and at night prepared suppers for their families, with no sheltering tents; and then made their beds in and under wagons that contained their earthly all.

How frequently, with intense sympathy and admiration, I watched the mother, when, forgetful of her own fatigue and destitution, she took unwearied pains to fix up, in the most palatable form, the allotted portion of food, and as she dealt it out was cheering the hearts of her homeless children, while, as I truly believed, her own was lifted to God in fervent prayer that their lives might be preserved, and, above all, that they might honor him in the religion for which she was an exile from the

[1]Eliza R. Snow traveled west with Stephen L. Markham and his wife and family.

home once sacred to her, for the sake of those precious ones that God had committed to her care. We were living on rations—our leaders having counseled that arrangement, to prevent an improvident use of provision that would result in extreme destitution.

Tullidge, *The Women of Mormondom*, pp. 311-12.

ELIZA R. SNOW

"We Were Prepared to Appreciate"

On the 2nd of August Brother Markham arrived from the East with teams; and on the 19th we bade good-bye to Mount Pisgah. Brother M. was' minus one teamster, and as Mrs. M. and I were to constitute the occupants of one wagon, with a gentle yoke of oxen, she proposed to drive. But, soon after we started, she was taken sick, and, of course, the driving fell to me. Had it been a horse-team I should have been amply qualified, but driving oxen was entirely a new business; however, I took the whip and very soon learned to "haw and gee," and acquitted myself, as teamster, quite honorably, driving most of the way to Winter Quarters. The cattle were so well trained that I could sit and drive. At best, however, it was fatiguing—the family being all sick by turns, and at times I had to cook, as well as nurse the sick; all of which I was thankful for strength to perform.

On the 27th we crossed the Missouri at Council Bluffs, and the next day came up with the general camp at Winter Quarters. From exposure and hardship I was taken sick soon after with a slow fever that terminated in chills and fever, and as I lay sick in my wagon, where my bed was exposed to heavy autumnal rains, and sometimes wet nearly from head to foot, I realized that I was near the gate of death; but my trust was in God, and his power preserved me. Many were sick around us, and no one could be properly cared for under the circumstances. Although, as before stated, I was exposed to the heavy rains while in the wagon, worse was yet to come.

On the 28th a company, starting out for supplies, required the wagon that Sister M. and I had occupied; and the log house we moved into was but partly chinked and mudded, leaving large crevices for the wind—then cold and blustering. This hastily erected hut was roofed on one side, with a tent-cloth thrown over the other, and, withal, was minus a chimney. A fire, which was built on one side, filled the house with smoke until it became unendurable. Sister Markham had partially recovered from her illness, but was quite feeble. I was not able to sit up much, and, under those circumstances, not at all, for the fire had to be dispensed with. Our cooking was done out of doors until after the middle of November, when a chimney was made, the house enclosed, and other improvements added, which we were prepared to appreciate.

Tullidge, *The Women of Mormondom,* pp. 315-17.

ELIZA R. SNOW

"Our Wild Mountain Home"

Our first winter in the mountains [Salt Lake City] was delightful; the ground froze but little; our coldest weather was three or four days in November, after which the men plowed and sowed, built houses, etc. The weather seemed to have been particularly ordered to met our very peculiar circumstances. Every labor, such as cultivating the ground, procuring fuel and timber from the canyons, etc., was a matter of experiment. Most of us were houseless; and what the result would have been, had that winter been like the succeeding ones, may well be conjectured.

President Young had kindly made arrangements for me to live with his wife, Clara Decker, who came with the pioneers and was living in a log-house about eighteen feet square, which constituted a portion of the east side of our fort. This hut, like most of those built the first year, was roofed with willows and earth, the roof having but little pitch, the first-comers having adopted the idea that the valley was subject to little if any rain, and our roofs were nearly flat. We suffered no inconvenience from this fact until about the middle of March, when a long storm of snow, sleet, and rain occurred, and for several days the sun did not make its appearance. The roof of our dwelling was covered deeper with earth than the adjoining ones; consequently it did not leak so soon, and some of my neighbors huddled in for shelter; but one evening, when several were socially sitting around, the water commenced dripping in one place, and then in another; they dodged it for awhile, but it increased so rapidly that they finally concluded they might as well go to their own wet houses. After they had gone I spread my umbrella over my head and shoulders as I ensconced myself in bed, the lower part of which, not shielded by the umbrella, was wet enough before morning. The earth overhead was thoroughly saturated, and after it commenced to drip, the storm was much worse indoors than out.

The small amount of breadstuff brought over the plains was sparingly dealt out; and our beef, made of cows and oxen which had constituted our teams, was, before it had time to fatten on the dry mountain grass, very inferior. Those to whom it yielded sufficient fat to grease their griddles were considered particularly fortunate. But we were happy in the rich blessings of peace, which, in the spirit of brotherly and sisterly union, we mutually enjoyed in our wild mountain home.

Tullidge, The Women of Mormondom, pp. 350-51.

Biographical Sketch

BELLE S. SPAFFORD

"**A** lifetime of service to women" best epitomizes the character and contributions of Belle S. Spafford. She has been general president of the Relief Society of The Church of Jesus Christ of Latter-day Saints since April 1945, and during this quarter-century of service has earned the love and respect of women in and out of the Church.

She has fulfilled well her responsibilities as wife and mother, and still has found time to devote to the challenging responsibilities of Church and community service.

Her devoted service to women has not been confined to the Church, for she has been a member of the National Advisory Committee to the White House Conference on Aging, and has served for many years in responsible positions in the National Council of Women. This organization of dedicated women honored her in 1968 by electing her to a two-year term as national president. She currently is an honorary member of the Executive Committee and chairman of the Constitutional Revisions Committee. Mrs. Spafford has also been active on the American Mothers Committee, Inc., presently serving as a vice-president.

She has been honored many times by educational, institutions and groups for her service to women, and is a spokesman for women now as she serves on the board of trustees of Brigham Young University.

She is a charming, gracious woman whose attainments have all come by merit during a useful, productive life.

Belle S. Spafford, *Women in Today's World* (Salt Lake City: Deseret Book Co., 1971).

BELLE S. SPAFFORD

"I Think I Would Choose Influence"

While there are a few women who hold positions of power today, it is my opinion that in world and national affairs women rule, in the main, by influence, while men rule by power. I recall at one time when I first served in a Relief Society presidency, the ward had built a new meetinghouse and they had to raise a few thousand dollars more in order to have it dedicated on the date scheduled. Relief Society was called upon to prepare and serve a turkey dinner to a large group. It was the first dinner in the new meetinghouse. We found the kitchen to be insufferably small. The women were in each other's way, slowing up the service. One woman fainted from the heat. The next day, in distress over this circumstance, I went to see the bishop. I explained the situation and requested that they knock out one wall and extend the kitchen to include the adjoining space which had been allocated to a classroom. He responded with sharpness. "Certainly not," he said, "we aren't going to start remodeling this building before it is dedicated," and he summarily dismissed me.

On my way home, discouraged and feeling somewhat reprimanded, I called at the home of one of the older sisters, and I poured forth my troubles. I concluded by saying, "In this church men have all the power; the women are just helpless." To this she replied, "Oh, no, my dear, the women are not helpless." Then she added, "If someone came to you, Sister Spafford, and had a good but different gift in each hand, and one was power and the other was influence and you had a choice, which gift would you choose?" I thought of this seriously for a moment and then I said, "I think I would choose influence." "You probably did, my dear," she said. "Influence is a great gift of God to women." Then she said, "Appreciate it and use it aright. Do not covet that which has been given to the brethren." This was a great lesson which I have never forgotten. I commend it to you young women in your companionships, in your homes, and in your church and community life.

"Woman in Today's World," BYU *Speeches of the Year*, March 3, 1970, p. 5.

BELLE S. SPAFFORD

"At My Mother's Knee"

I recall that several years ago when Relief Society sisters were studying the Book of Mormon every sister was expected to read the book in its entirety. As a special feature of the general conference and to encourage the sisters in their efforts, a brother was invited to speak to them on the subject of the Book of Mormon. Last-minute circumstances, however, made it impossible for him to attend the conference. It became necessary to obtain another speaker the morning of the day on which the address was scheduled. Elder Matthew Cowley was enlisted. He delivered a masterful address, in which he bore this impressive testimony:

"I would like to bear my testimony to you about the book which you are studying in Relief Society, the Book of Mormon. I know nothing about archaeology. I have not studied the maps which apparently relate to the Book of Mormon, the travels of the Lehites, the Lamanites, and so forth. I know very little about the outside evidences of the Book of Mormon, but I have a testimony of the divinity of this book, and that testimony has come to me from within the two covers of the book itself." ("Testimony Through Reading the Book of Mormon," *The Relief Society Magazine,* January 1953, pp. 7-8.)

In appreciation I said to Brother Cowley, "I marvel that you could give such a magnificent and convincing address with so little time in which to prepare!" To this Brother Cowley responded, "What do you mean by little time in which to prepare? I had plenty of time. I have had a lifetime. My preparation for that address began when I was a little boy at my mother's knee."

Spafford, *Women in Today's World,* pp. 43-44.

BELLE S. SPAFFORD

"*Mother Would Take Time to Help*"

I know of one young mother whose familiarity with and love for the scriptures came to her largely after her marriage to a returned missionary. So meaningful did they become in her life that she has conscientiously devoted herself to helping her children to know and appreciate them.

227

Today her ten-year-old girl and eight-year-old boy have their own copies of the standard works. At first, as very little ones, they were provided with illustrated stories from the Bible and Book of Mormon. Mother read these to the children.

Later the children, as they learned to read, would read the stories back to mother. Then as they read from their story book mother would read the same story, in whole or in part as the children were able to comprehend, from the scripture itself, explaining to the children the difference between the book from which she was reading and the story book from which they read. Always she emphasized the greater value of the scripture, implanting in the children a special regard for it. Later as the children became ready they would read to mother a familiar story from the scripture itself. It was then they were given their own volumes. When a simple verse had special meaning for the children, mother would take time to help them memorize it and mark it in their own books.

When the children are given opportunity to talk in Sunday School or other Church gatherings, they select their subject from their own books, with mother's interested help and guidance. The selection is usually a principle of the gospel such as prayer, Sabbath observance, or Word of Wisdom, rather than a story.

A regular practice in the home is for the father to inquire at dinner on Sunday, "What was your Sunday School lesson about?" Then after dinner the father makes a practice of helping the children find something about their lesson in their books. Mother teaches Primary. The children and their scriptures are brought actively into her lesson preparation. Thus acquaintance with the scripture has been handled in a way that has brought happy companionship with mother and father as well as light and truth into the lives of the children, along with an acquaintance with these great books.

In addition, the hours spent together with the word of the Lord are bound to develop a close family unity, which in itself will bring rich rewards.

Spafford, *Women in Today's World*, pp. 41-42.

"Pictures of the Best Things"

"**B**e ashamed to die until you have achieved some victory for humanity."—Horace Mann.

Someone has likened the mind to a closed room in which we live all of our lives. We walk about in this closed room day after day, year after year. On its walls we hang pictures representing our efforts. We naturally key our lives to these pictures. If we shut our minds in this dark room with only pictures of our weaknesses and our failures before us, we lose confidence in our own abilities, increase our weaknesses and our fears. Thus we lose our power to DO.

Why not then emphasize our *strengths?* Why not in this mind room hang pictures of the best things we have done, the successes that have been ours, holding before us the fine lessons we have given, the life we have enriched, the strengths we have developed. Think of all the things we have done of which we may be proud. What we have done we can do again with even greater success because of the experience behind us.

Latter-day Saints realize that our strengths are God-given. Our Father has told us that we cannot all have all gifts but that each is given his special gift and is expected to use it for the good of man.

"For all have not every gift given unto them; for there are many gifts, and to every man is given a gift by the Spirit of God.

"To some is given one, and to some is given another, that all may be profited thereby." (D&C 46:11-12.)

In recognizing that we have a strength, we take the first step in its development. The second step is putting it to active use. The Church provides abundant opportunity to put to use all of the strengths of all its members for the good of all mankind.

Spafford, *Women in Today's World*, pp. 125-26.

"Endure to the End"

May I relate an experience. Authorization, as many of you know, has been given by the Brethren for Relief Societies, under specified circumstances, to be organized in nursing or residential homes for older sisters. One day I visited such a Relief Society. The members were between seventy-five and ninety years of age. They were ambulatory, bright of mind, and enthusiastic over their society. The lesson was from the Doctrine and Covenants and was followed by testimony bearing. The sisters contributed intelligently to the lesson discussions. Their offerings reflected a knowledge of Church doctrine and familiarity with the gospel, as well as rich life experiences. It was a delightful meeting. Then came the testimony period. Each sister who spoke, one by one, prayed that she would endure to the end. As I contemplated their intelligent understanding of the gospel as demonstrated in the discussion, and as I considered how late in life it was for most of them, I thought, why would they pray that they might endure to the end? Surely they have already proved themselves.

Later, however, in private conversation with some of them, I was made aware that they were not entirely above reproach, that they had a tendency to excuse themselves for failures to comply with the laws of the gospel because of age and circumstances.

These are a few comments made by these sisters as I talked with them:

One sister said, "We have sacrament meeting here at the home, as well as Relief Society, but I never go to sacrament meeting. I am too old to be preached to." I inquired, "Don't you feel a need to partake of the sacrament?" "No," the sister indifferently replied. "I don't think it matters at my age."

Another sister said, "I want to move to a little better home.

I have enough money to do so. I have no one on whom to spend my money but myself. My family does not need it, and I am no longer interested in doing things for others that cost money. I don't even pay tithing. I don't think the Lord expects it of one my age."

Still another sister, who was drinking tea as I called, said, "I almost live on tea. When I was a younger woman, you couldn't have hired me to drink a cup of tea, but I don't think it will be held against me now."

Yet another said, as we heard footsteps near the door, "I hope that's not my daughter. She only comes because she fears criticism if she doesn't. She has very little love for me, and I have very little for her."

One more comment: "I seem to be growing weaker every day, suffering as I do with pain. I used to have the elders administer to me, but I don't believe in that anymore."

Attendance at sacrament meeting, partaking of the sacrament, renewing one's covenants, the payment of tithing, observance of the Word of Wisdom, love of family, priesthood administration—all basic laws of the gospel—had been abandoned by one or the other of these sisters with a feeling of justification; yet each had earnestly prayed that she might endure to the end.

Sympathetic as we may be toward these sisters and toward their circumstances, and understanding as we may be of their actions, yet we must recognize that with clear minds they were justifying the nonobservance of God's laws. I am led to ask also, Has the Lord ever set a retirement age for keeping his commandments?

Spafford, *Women in Today's World*, pp. 46-47.

CATHERINE CURTIS
SPENCER *

"Charge Them to Obey the Gospel"

Catherine Curtis Spencer died on the 12th of March, 1846, at Indian Creek near Keosaqua, Iowa Territory, at the age of thirty-five years, wanting nine days.

In one month from the time of her departure from Illinois to the wilderness, she fell a victim to the cares and hardships of persecution. The youngest daughter of a numerous family, brought up in affluence and nurtured with fondness and peculiar care, as the favorite of her father's house, her slender yet healthy frame could not withstand the inclemency of the winter season (the thermometer below zero for ten days). The change from warm rooms of brick and plastered walls, to that of mere canvas ceiling and roof, floored with snow and icy earth, was too much for her fragile form to endure. When, through unforeseen hindrances in traveling, there was no place where sleep could visit, or food suited to the demands of nature be administered to her or her six little children, from the age of thirteen and under, she

---

°Catherine Curtis Spencer, was the courageous wife of Orson Spencer. She was the mother of six children, one of whom is the author of this story—Aurelia Spencer Rogers, who was the first general Primary president in the Church.

would cheer her little innocents with the songs of Zion. The melody of her rare voice, like the harmony and confluence of many virtues in her mind, contributed on that memorable epoch of the Church, to render her the glory of her husband and the solace and joy of her children. . . .

Under the influence of a severe cold, she gradually wasted away, telling her children from time to time how she wanted them to live, and conduct themselves, when they should become motherless and pilgrims in a strange land. To her companion she would sometimes say, "I think you will have to give me up and let me go." As her little ones would often inquire at the door of the wagon, "How is mamma? Is she any better?" she would turn to her husband, who sat by her side endeavoring to keep the severities of rain and cold from her, with, "Oh, you dear little children, how I do hope you may fall into kind hands when I am gone!" A night or two before she died she said to her husband, with unwonted animation, "A heavenly messenger has appeared to me tonight and told me that I had done and suffered enough, and that he had now come to convey me to a mansion of gold."

Soon after, she said she wished her husband to call her children and her friends to her bedside, that she might give them a parting kiss; which, being done, she said to her companion, "I love you more than ever, but you must let me go. I only want to live for your sake and that of our children." When asked if she had anything to say to her father's family, she replied emphatically, "Charge them to obey the gospel."

The rain continued so incessantly for many days and nights that it was impossible to keep her bedding dry or comfortable, and for the first time she uttered a desire to be in a house. The request might have moved a heart of adamant. Immediately a man by the name of Barnes, living not far from the camp, consented to have her brought to his house, where she died in peace with a smile upon her countenance.

Nibley, *Exodus to Greatness*, pp. 133-34.

PRISCILLA MOGRIDGE STAINES *

"The Elder Had to Chop a Hole in the Ice"

I was brought up in the Episcopal faith from my earliest childhood, my parents being members of the Episcopal Church. But as my mind became matured, and I thought more about religion, I became dissatisfied with the doctrines taught by that church, and I prayed to God my Heavenly Father to direct me aright, that I might know the true religion.

Shortly after being thus concerned about my salvation, I heard Mormonism and believed it. God had sent the true gospel to me in answer to my prayer.

It was a great trial for a young maiden (I was only nineteen years of age) to forsake all for the gospel—father, mother, brothers and sisters—and to leave my childhood's home and native land, never expecting to see it again. This was the prospect before me. The Saints were already leaving the fatherland, in obedience to the doctrine of gathering, which was preached at this time with great plainness by the elders as an imperative

*Priscilla Mogridge Staines was born in Widbrook, England, on March 11, 1823, a daughter of John and Mary Crook Mogridge. After her conversion she immigrated to America to join the Saints in Nauvoo.

234

command of God. We looked upon the gathering as necessary to our salvation. Nothing of our duty in this respect was concealed, and we were called upon to emigrate to America as soon as the way should open, to share the fate of the Saints, whatever might come. Young as I was and alone of all my family in the faith, I was called to take up my cross and lay my earthly all upon the altar; yet so well satisfied was I with my new religion that I was willing to make every sacrifice for it in order to gain my salvation and prove myself not unworthy of the Saints' reward.

Having determined to be baptized, I resolved to at once obey the gospel, although it was midwinter and the weather bitterly cold.

It is proper to here state that baptism was a trial to the converts in England in those days. They had to steal away, even unknown to their friends oftentimes, and scarcely daring to tell the Saints themselves that they were about to take up the cross; and not until the ordinance had been administered, and the Holy Ghost gave them boldness, could they bring themselves to proclaim openly that they had cast in their lot with the despised Mormons. Nor was this all, for generally the elders had to administer baptism when the village was wrapt in sleep, lest persecutors should gather a mob to disturb the solemn scene with gibes and curses, accompanied with stones or clods of earth torn from the river bank and hurled at the disciple and minister during the performance of the ceremony.

On the evening of a bitterly cold day in midwinter, as before stated, I walked four miles to the house of a local elder for baptism. Arriving at his house, we waited until midnight, in order that the neighbors might not disturb us, and then repaired to a stream of water a quarter of a mile away. Here we found the water, as we anticipated, frozen over, and the elder had to chop a hole in the ice large enough for the purpose of baptism. It was a scene and an occasion I shall never forget. Memory today brings back the emotions and sweet awe of that moment. None but God and his angels, and the few witnesses who stood on the bank with us, heard my covenant; but in the solemnity of that midnight hour it seemed as though all nature were listening, and the recording angel writing our words in the book of the Lord. Is it strange that such a scene, occurring in the life of a Latter-day Saint, should make an everlasting impression, as this did on mine?

Having been thus baptized, I returned to the house in my wet and freezing garments.

Up to this hour, as intimated, my heart's best affection had been centered on home, and my greatest mental struggle in obeying the gospel had been over the thought of soon leaving that home; but no sooner had I emerged from the water, on that night of baptism, and received my confirmation at the water's edge, than I became filled with an irresistible desire to join the Saints who were gathering to America. . . .

Tullidge, *The Women of Mormondom*, pp. 285-91.

PRISCILLA MOGRIDGE STAINES

"The Prophet Joseph at First Sight"

Shortly thereafter [December 27th, 1843], I left the home of my birth to gather to Nauvoo. I was alone. It was a dreary winter day on which I went to Liverpool and saw the ocean that would soon roll between me and all I loved; my heart almost failed me. But . . . there was no turning back. I remembered the words of the Savior: "He that leaveth not father and mother, brother and sister, for my sake, is not worthy of me," and I believed his promise to those who forsook all for his sake; so I thus alone set out for the reward of everlasting life, trusting in God.

In company with two hundred and fifty Saints I embarked

on the sailing vessel *Fanny,* and after a tedious passage of six weeks' duration, we arrived in New Orleans. There an unexpected difficulty met us. The steamer *Maid of Iowa,* belonging to the Prophet Joseph, and on which the company of Saints had expected to ascend the Mississippi to Nauvoo, was embargoed and lashed to the wharf. But Providence came to our aid. A lady of fortune was in the company—a Mrs. Bennett—and out of her private purse she not only lifted the embargo, but also fitted out the steamer with all necessary provisions, fuel, etc., and soon the company were again on their way. . . .

As the *Maid of Iowa* had made slow progress, and had been frequently passed by more swift-going steamers, her progress was well known by the friends of Nauvoo. So on the day of our arrival the Saints were out en masse to welcome us. I had never before seen any of those assembled, yet I felt certain, as the boat drew near, that I should be able to pick out the Prophet Joseph at first sight. This belief I communicated to Mrs. Bennett, whose acquaintance I had made on the voyage. She wondered at it; but I felt impressed by the Spirit that I should know him. As we neared the pier the Prophet was standing among the crowd. At the moment, however, I recognized him according to the impression, and pointed him out to Mrs. Bennett, with whom I was standing alone on the hurricane deck.

Scarcely had the boat touched the pier when, singularly enough, Joseph sprang on board, and, without speaking with anyone, made his way direct to where we were standing, and addressing Mrs. Bennett by name, thanked her kindly for lifting the embargo from his boat, and blessed her for so materially aiding the Saints.

Tullidge, *The Women of Mormondom,* pp. 285-91.

EMMELINE B. WELLS*

"The Mantle of the Prophet Fell Upon Brigham Young"

I feel that I have a testimony to bear, that I have always kept from the very day that I entered the City of Nauvoo and saw the Prophet Joseph. He came down to the boat to meet the Saints who were coming from the eastern states and the middle states up to the West.

I had been baptized by the wish of my mother, who became a Latter-day Saint as soon as she heard the gospel, but I had no testimony and I had not very much faith, because I did not know much about things. . . .

When I came up the river on the boat, and standing on the top of the boat to see the Prophet on the landing from the boat, I knew instantly then that the gospel was true by the feeling that

---

°Emmeline Blanche Wells, the fifth general president of the Relief Society, was born February 29, 1828, at Petersham, Worcester County, Massachusetts, a daughter of David Woodward and Diadama Hare. She was married to Newel K. Whitney in 1845; he died in 1850. In 1852 she was married to Daniel H. Wells. From 1876 to 1914 she edited the *Women's Exponent.* Two books of her poetry were also published. The mother of six children, she died April 25, 1921. At her funeral in the Salt Lake Tabernacle, attended by 6,000 persons, President Charles W. Penrose paid the following tribute: "There was no selfishness in her soul nor in her work; her hand reached out to the entire world."

pervaded me from the crown of my head to the end of my fingers and toes, and every part of my body. I was sure then that I was right, that "Mormonism" was true and that I was fully paid for all the sacrifices that I had made to come to Nauvoo. I felt that just to see him would be worth it all. I had been prepared in a measure for seeing him, but I want to tell you I was not disappointed, because there never was a man like him.

The only incident where a man resembled him was when Brigham Young announced himself as president of the Church and the successor of the Prophet Joseph. I don't remember the words, but that was the announcement that he made in the grove on Temple Hill in the city of Nauvoo. There were but few people that knew he had come. They knew all the Twelve were away at the time that the Prophet Joseph and his brother Hyrum were slain, and I think very few in that audience knew that Brigham Young had returned. When he came forward and made that announcement, the whole company arose and exclaimed, in one voice, you might say, that it was the Prophet Joseph.

I was standing in a wagon box on wheels, so I did not have to rise, but those who were seated arose and made that exclamation. I could see very well, and every one of them thought it was really the Prophet Joseph risen from the dead. But after Brigham Young had spoken a few words, the tumult subsided, and the people really knew that it was not the Prophet Joseph, but the President of the Quorum of the Twelve Apostles. It was the most wonderful manifestation, I think, that I have ever known or seen, and I have seen a very great number. . . .

I wanted particularly to tell you of the manifestation when the mantle of the Prophet fell upon Brigham Young. After that we had the greatest faith in him, the greatest that could possibly be; and we have had great faith in all those who have followed him.

Nibley, *Faith-Promoting Stories*, pp. 137-38, 140.

LOUISA WELLS*

"Wet to the Skin"

The next year many of the pioneers made their second journey to the mountains, and with them now came Daniel H. Wells, the story of whose wife, Louisa, shall close these journeys of the pioneers.

Although exceedingly desirous of crossing the plains with the first company of that year, her father was unable to do more than barely provide the two wagons necessary to carry his family and provisions, and the requisite number of oxen to draw them. The luxury of an extra teamster to care for the second wagon was out of the question; and so Louisa, although but twenty-two years of age, and although she had never driven an ox in her life, heroically undertook the task of driving one of the outfits, and caring for a younger brother and sister.

The picture of her starting is somewhat amusing. After seeing that her allotment of baggage and provisions, along with her little brother and sister, had been stowed in the wagon, with

---

*Louisa Wells was the first wife of Daniel H. Wells, a counselor to President Brigham Young in the First Presidency. She was twenty-two years of age when she crossed the plains with her husband. She was well-known throughout Utah in assisting the sick and needy and was loved by many people.

a capacious old-fashioned sunbonnet on her head, a parasol in one hand and an ox-whip in the other, she placed herself by the side of her leading yoke of oxen and bravely set her face westward. Matters went well enough for a short distance, considering her inexperience with oxen; but the rain began to pour, and shortly her parasol was found to be utterly inadequate, so in disgust she threw it into the wagon and traveled on in the wet grass 'mid the pouring rain. Presently the paste-board stiffeners of her sunbonnet began to succumb to the persuasive moisture, and before night, bedraggled and muddy, and thoroughly wet to the skin, her appearance was fully as forlorn as her condition was pitiable.

This was truly a discouraging start, but nothing daunted, she pressed on with the company, and never allowed her spirits to flag.

Tullidge, *The Women of Mormondom*, pp. 336-37.

SUSANNAH WHITE

"I Don't Need to Be Afraid of a Praying Indian"

The first sawmill in Escalante, Utah, was situated in North Creek Canyon, about fourteen miles from town. This mill was built and managed by Henry J. White.

One Sunday it became necessary for Mr. White to leave his young wife, Susannah, alone at the sawmill until the next day. He disliked doing this because Indians were camped close by, and one . . . was known to be the meanest Indian in the country.

About two hours after Mr. White left, this very Indian came to the mill. He rode up to the cabin and said, "Where is your Mormon?" Susannah pretended that she wasn't frightened, and told the Indian that Mr. White was in town. He said he wanted to hunt above the mill, so Susannah told him to go. He rode away, but reappeared in the late afternoon with two deer tied on his horse, and again asked, "Where is your Mormon?" She told him he was still in town. The Indian then asked to stay all night. She told him he could stay and for him to put his horse in the corral and feed it.

The deer were hung in a nearby tree and the horse cared for before the Indian came to the cabin. Susannah had supper ready when he came in, and after eating, they sat by the fire-place. He tried to tell her the town news and passed her a little dirty sack of pine nuts.

While sitting there the Indian asked, "You 'fraid?"

"No, I'm not afraid," replied Susannah. "I can shoot as good as any Indian."

The reply amused the Indian and laughingly he replied, "You no shoot Indian."

When the time came to retire, Susannah gave him some matches and said, "My Mormon always makes the fire in the morning." She then gave him a quilt and some rugs to make himself a bed by the fire.

Susannah, thinking she would have to remain awake all night and watch him, just slipped off her shoes and went to bed. When she looked around, she was amazed to see the Indian kneeling in prayer by the side of his bed.

Susannah had been terribly frightened all evening, but seeing the Indian now she said to herself, "I don't need to be afraid of a praying Indian." Soon after, she went to sleep and slept until next morning, when she was awakened by the Indian, who was building the fire. He insisted on helping milk the cows, but she explained that the cows would be afraid of him; but she told him he could cut her an armful of wood, which he gladly did. He cut a large pile instead of an armful.

After they had eaten breakfast, the Indian left. But before going, he cut two hind quarters off one of the deer and left them hanging in the tree for her.

Children's Friend, September 1943, p. 443.

ELIZABETH ANN WHITNEY*

"The Gift Would Never Leave Her"

Elizabeth, familiarly known as Mother Whitney, was baptized in November 1830, less than a year after the organization of the Church, and from that time to her death, she was a faithful, loyal church member.

Among her gifts was . . . the gift of tongues, which she always exercised in singing. The Prophet Joseph Smith promised her that if she kept the faith, the gift would never leave her, and it never did. On one occasion, at a meeting held in the Kirtland Temple, Sister Whitney sang in tongues and Parley P. Pratt interpreted the song as a hymn descriptive of the different dispensations from Adam to the present age. She last exercised the sweet and holy influence of her gift at a party given by Emmeline B. Wells in honor of Mother Whitney's eighty-first birthday.

*Elizabeth Ann Whitney was born on December 26, 1800, in Derby, New Haven County, Connecticut, a daughter of Gibson Smith and Polly Bradley. She was married to Newel K. Whitney October 20, 1822. She served as second counselor to Emma Smith, wife of the Prophet, in the Relief Society in Nauvoo. She served as president of the central board of Relief Society in Utah. The Whitneys emigrated to Salt Lake Valley with the Saints; Bishop Whitney died in 1850. The mother of eleven children, she died February 15, 1883. The Prophet Joseph Smith referred to her as the "Sweetest Songstress of Zion."

She also brought blessings to many of the daughters of Zion by her service in the House of the Lord from the time she received her endowments. . . .

Outstanding though her accomplishments were, Mother Whitney was most greatly blessed in her children. Her oldest sons, Horace and Orson, were among the original Utah pioneers of 1847. . . . Another son, H. K. Whitney, was the father of the apostle Orson F. Whitney.

LDS Biographical Encyclopedia, vol. 3, pp. 563-64.

Biographical Sketch

ANNA WIDTSOE

Anna Karine Gaarden Widtsoe was born June 4, 1849, in the little fishing village of Titran on the little island of Fröya, the outermost island off the coast of Norway. Her father was Peder Olsen Gaarden, and her mother was Beret Martha Haavig.

Anna Gaarden was married to John Andersen Widtsoe on December 29, 1870. She was twenty-one years old, and he was nine years older. Her husband died in 1878. At the time of his death she had two sons: John Andreas, age six, and Osborne, who was only two months old.

Anna Widtsoe studied the gospel and investigated the Church for two years and was baptized in 1881. She left Norway to emigrate to Utah October 20, 1883. She and her two sons made their home in Logan, Utah. Anna worked and supported her sons, and they both received fine educations. Osborne was a professor of English at the University of Utah and John was president of that same institution prior to his call to the Council of the Twelve.

Anna Widtsoe fulfilled a mission to Norway with her sister as her companion. She passed away on July 11, 1919, in Salt

Lake City at seventy years of age. On the day of her funeral, Elder John A. Widtsoe wrote the following tribute to his mother in his diary: "She was a most devoted mother, loyal to the last degree. Her devotion to the cause of truth was almost sublime. She was self-sacrificing beyond expression in behalf of her own and those who needed help. Her mind was transparently clear. The great issues of her life always swept before her. To her I owe my inspiration. Thanks! Many thanks! dear Mother. Good-bye, until we meet again. . . ."

John A. Widtsoe, *In the Gospel Net* (Salt Lake City: Bookcraft, 1966), p. 130.

ANNA WIDTSOE

"A Mormon Tract Was Stuffed Into Each Shoe"

One day [Anna Widtsoe] asked a neighbor, a ship's captain living in the same house, an older resident, to recommend a shoemaker to whom she might take her son's shoes for repair. One Olaus Johnsen, a very competent, honest workman, was recommended. In fact, the shoemaker's son Arnt brought to the house a pair of the captain's shoes, and took with him for repair, a pair of John's shoes. When the boy's shoes were returned, a Mormon tract was stuffed into each shoe. A little later with a parcel containing another pair of old shoes, the widow set forth in the warm sunshine of the spring of 1879 for the half-hour walk to Johnsen's shoemaker shop. It certainly did not occur to her that she was making the most fateful visit of her life. Yet, who can say that it was the most fateful. The events of life are like the threads of a tapestry—all together make the pattern and picture.

Olaus Johnsen was a wholesome, well-spoken man in his forties, a workman who knew his craft. His wife was of the sturdy Norwegian type. Anna Widtsoe first met the wife, and made inquiry about the meaning of the tracts found in her son's shoes that had been returned, repaired. Mrs. Johnsen declared that they told the truth, but that Mr. Johnsen would explain the whole matter.

The shoemaker agreed to put soles on the shoes, strong enough to last a good while even under the wear of a lively, active lad, who was always moving about. The details of business were soon agreed upon; the commonplaces of courteous people were exchanged; the widow was about to leave the shop, yet a little curious about the tracts which she had found in the first pair of shoes when they were returned, but unwilling to ask too many questions.

Anna Widtsoe's hand was on the door latch, when the shoemaker said, somewhat hesitatingly, for the business was concluded and the lady was a stranger, "You may be surprised to hear me say that I can give you something of more value than soles for your child's shoes." She was surprised. She looked into the eyes of the man, who stood straight and courageous in his shop.

"What can you, a shoemaker, give me better than soles for my son's shoes? You speak in riddles," she answered.

The shoemaker did not hesitate. "If you will but listen, I can teach you the Lord's true plan of salvation for his children. I can teach you how to find happiness in this life, and to prepare for eternal joy in the life to come. I can tell you whence you came, why you are upon earth, and where you will go after death. I can teach you, as you have never known it before, the love of God for his children on earth."

Understanding, happiness, joy, love—the words with which she was wrestling! But, this was a shoemaker shop. This man was clearly a humble man who knew little of the wisdom of schools and churches. She felt confused. She simply asked, "Who are you?"

"I am a member of the Church of Christ—we are called Mormons. We have the truth of God."

Mormons! It was terrible. She had innocently walked into a dangerous place. Hurriedly she thanked the shoemaker, left the shop, and climbed the hill.

Yet, as she walked homeward, the words of the shoemaker rang in her ears; and she remembered a certain power in his voice and majesty in his bearing when he delivered his message and bore his testimony. He was a shoemaker, but no ordinary man. Could it really be that the Mormons had the truth of the Lord? No, it was absurd! But, it made her thoughtful and restless. When the repaired shoes were brought to the house a day or two later, by the shoemaker's young son, Arnt Johnsen, Anna Widtsoe found, carefully tucked into each shoe, other Mormon tracts. The shoemaker was valiant. He missed no opportunity to fulfill the obligation of a Latter-day Saint, to bear witness modestly and properly but steadily, to all the world.

Then began two years of struggle.

The tracts in the shoes aroused her curiosity to the extent that one Sunday she went to a Mormon meeting. The meeting room was on the second floor of the shoemaker's home, a sturdy log house. A small group of people were there; and a fiery speaker, a missionary, raised all manner of questions in her mind. The main effect of that meeting was a resentment against the primitive environment of the meeting, and the quality of the people who were present. Very humble people constituted the membership of the Trondhjem Branch. Class distinctions were sharply drawn in the land. Anna Widtsoe, though a fishermaiden, had been well born, in the economic as well as in the moral sense; and she had moved upward with the years. She was now of the professional class. To join such a group as she saw there that Sunday seemed to her tradition-bound mind to be a step downward. One day, some months later, when the truth was forcing itself upon her, she came home, stood quietly in the middle of the floor, and said aloud, to herself, "Must I step down to that? Yes, if it is the truth, I must do so."

Soon, however, all else was forgotten in her battles with the shoemaker and the missionaries upon points of doctrine. She knew her Bible. Time upon time she came prepared to vanquish the elders, only to meet defeat herself. She had not read the Bible as these men did. Gradually she began to comprehend that her reading had been colored and overshadowed by the teachings of the church of her childhood; and that these men, these Mormon missionaries, accepted the Bible in a truer, more literal manner. She liked it. Nevertheless she fought fearlessly. It was no use. At length she had to admit that the Bible was all on the side of the Mormons.

Even then she was not ready. There were other matters to be settled. Questions of authority, revelation, life within the church, and a hundred others that her quick mind formulated, were presented to the missionaries, debated, discussed and taken up again. She had a worthy teacher in the missionary then in Trondhjem, Elder Anthon L. Skanchy, whose knowledge of the gospel was extensive and sound, and whose wisdom in leading inquirers to truth was unusually fine. This well-informed, intelligent widow tested his powers. Upon her he directed the full battery of gospel evidence. Unwillingly, yet prayerfully, she became convinced that she was in the presence of eternal truth.

At length, on April 1, 1881, a little more than two years after she first heard the gospel, she was baptized into the Church by Elder Anthon L. Skanchy. Thin ice still lay over the edges of the fjord, which had to be broken to permit the ordinance to be performed. The water was icy cold. Yet, she declared to her dying day that never before in all her life had she felt warmer or more comfortable than when she came out of the baptismal waters of old Trondhjem's fjord. The fire within was kindled, never to be extinguished. The humble people of the branch became her brethren and sisters. She loved them, and rejoiced in their company.

Widtsoe, *In the Gospel Net,* pp. 53-57.

"The Sound of the Daily Mail Cart"

As told by John A. Widtsoe

Two months before we were to sail from Oslo, I was sent to my father's oldest sister, who with her husband lived in the country some twenty-five miles north of Oslo. There I spent happy weeks among the fields and forests on the two large estates that my uncle was managing.

My aunt was scandalized that any member of the family had become besmirched with Mormonism. She was determined to prevent the oldest son of her beloved brother from going to Utah. . . . Therefore, she arranged that a few days before my mother's expected arrival, I was to be sent into the mountain districts, so far away that I could not be brought back in time for the sailing of the boat. And should the stubborn mother miss the boat to recover her son, no one would know where her son was. It was a perfect plan, which, of course, was unknown to me. I understood only that I was going into the mountains for an outing.

The day for my departure came. My belongings were all packed. The horses were at the door. We were at breakfast. Suddenly there was the sound of the daily mail cart, which also carried passengers. It stopped in front of the house. Out stepped my mother with my brother Osborne, just one week earlier than the set date! My aunt's consternation was inexpressible. Even now I must smile at the episode. Yet, even then, my aunt wanted to take me into the mountains, "for a change." She also was of the stern kind. But my mother was unyielding. "We leave for Oslo this afternoon." Thus, I was not kidnapped, and another "best-laid" plan was foiled. Why my mother left her home a week early she could not explain. "I just had to leave then." So the Lord guides his faithful children.

John A. Widtsoe, *In a Sunlit Land* (Salt Lake City: Deseret News Press, 1952), pp. 7-8.

"Sister Widtsoe Is Not a Beggar, Yet"

It was pride, foolish pride, perhaps, rather than necessity, that on several occasions led the little family in those early days to the brink of want. In the spring of 1884 Anna Widtsoe moved into a two-room house—a noble rise in fortune—nearer the business center and in another ward so that her customers would not have so far to go. Collections were slow one month; John was out of work. At last the family had only a sack of "shorts" left. For three weeks, they lived on "shorts" and water. Never before, in man's history, had "shorts" been served in so many different dishes as the widow's ingenuity devised. Nevertheless, the diet was frightfully monotonous. They did not know, then, the high nutritive value of "shorts."

One day, after nearly three weeks of rations on "shorts" and water, the Sixth Ward had a ward reunion. A Mormon ward re-union includes a feast of all the good things of earth, or nearly all. When the meal was ended, there was food left over, and the good-hearted Bishop Skanchy—and no man was ever kinder to the poor—filled a large basket with roast chicken and lamb, vegetables and bread, cakes and desserts, and sent them by a messenger to the widow and her sons, who now lived in the First Ward.

When the "shorts"-filled boys saw the well-filled basket of goodies uncovered upon their table, there was eager, anticipat-ing swallowing, and much inward joy; all of which was changed to darkest despair when the widow drew herself up to her full height and said, "Brother, please take the basket back to the bishop with my thanks, and say to him that Sister Widtsoe is not a beggar, yet." To the boys, the departure of that basket with its contents was the darkest moment of their first years in Zion. It seemed a foolish pride, but perhaps it was better for the family to nurse a stubborn independence.

Widtsoe, *In the Gospel Net*, pp. 67-68.

"Get Behind Me, Satan"

She [Anna Widtsoe] had not been taught the Word of Wisdom, except as it had been mentioned casually in her gospel conversations. Now she began to understand its real meaning and purpose and the necessity of obeying it, as it was the desire of the Father that his children should heed it. Like nearly all of her country people she had drunk coffee from her childhood, and was an occasional user of tea. Alcoholic beverages she did not use. She set about to give up the use of tea and coffee, but found it difficult. When she sewed every night far beyond midnight, the cup of coffee seemed to freshen her, she thought. After a two months' struggle she came home one day, having given serious consideration to the Word of Wisdom problem. Her mind was made up. She stood in the middle of the room and said aloud, "Never again. Get behind me, Satan!" and walked briskly to her cupboard, took out the packages of coffee and tea, and threw them on the fire. From that day she never used tea or coffee.

Widtsoe, *In the Gospel Net,* p. 73.

"The Lord Had Given the Boys to Her"

Her house was not yet built when she decided that John must no longer be kept from regular schooling. He was well employed and giving satisfaction; soon he would be able to provide for the family. To take him out of such employment, to get a bit more book learning, considering that they were a family of poor immigrants, seemed very unwise to many good people. The bishop remonstrated with the widow. "The boy would become lazy. He should be in the canyon now, learning to do hard work. His boys were trained to work. She should be content with what she had." The widow listened politely, though the storm was gathering. She was never afraid to speak her mind when occasion arose. "She was grateful for the bishop's interest; he meant well. But, the Lord had given the boys to her and not to the bishop. They were her responsibility, not his. She had obligations to the living and the dead which he did not know about. Besides, he did not understand, as she did, that the training of the mind is as necessary as the training of the muscles. She concluded by looking into the future, and predicting that he and others would yet admit that she was right; and that the time would come when all children would be given the opportunity of higher education." The good man, for he was a kind, generous man, limited in his vision by his own hard pioneer experience, saw that nothing could be done to change the widow's mind, and that the boy would have to go on to possible destruction!

Widtsoe, *In the Gospel Net,* pp. 78-79.

"With Eyes Now Blazing"

The three years after the autumn of 1894 were happy ones. The widow kept house for her two sons. . . .

During this time, as always, she was firm in her devotion to the gospel. The eternal truth restored through the Prophet Joseph Smith was the joy of her life. That faith she knew must be kept untarnished. That must be defended at all costs. She was everywhere the upholder of the Church, its principles and officers. At times this attitude was put to the test. For example:

About 1896, Moses Thatcher, an apostle of the Church, was suspended from service in the Quorum of the Twelve Apostles. Brother Thatcher, a man of unusual gifts and most charming personality, was very popular in his home town of Logan, as throughout the Church. His suspension caused widespread discussion, and many of his intimate Logan friends felt that he had been treated unjustly, and took his side against the action of the authorities of the Church. The temporary upheaval was tempestuous. Men's feelings ran high. While the excitement was at its height, two of the ward elders called at the Widtsoe home as ward teachers. The widow's two sons were home, and the whole family assembled to be instructed by the visiting teachers. Soon the visitors began to comment on the "Thatcher episode," as it was called, and explained how unjustly Brother Thatcher had been treated. The widow answered not a word, but there was a gathering storm in her stern eyes and high-held head.

After some minutes of listening to the visitors find fault with the Quorum of the Apostles with respect to Brother Thatcher, she slowly rose from her chair and as slowly walked to the entrance door of the house, which she threw wide open. With eyes now blazing she turned to the two brethren and said: "There is the door. I want you to leave this house instantly. I will not permit anyone in this house to revile the authorities of the Church, men laboring under divine inspiration. Nor do I wish such things spoken before my sons whom I have taught to love the leaders of the Church. And don't come back until you come in the right spirit to teach us the gospel. Here is the door. Now, go!" The visitors hurried out shamefacedly, for the widow had chastised them thoroughly. In defense of the gospel, Sister Widtsoe knew no fear.

Widtsoe, *In the Gospel Net*, pp. 97-98.

MAE R. WINTERS[*]

"The Apron"

One of the fondest memories that I have of my mother is her apron. She always wore one. It was a large straight affair gathered at the waist, with strings that fastened in the back and tied in a bow. The apron was very full. I am sure it had in it several yards of material, gingham or calico for everyday, and fine white lawn or linen, with handmade lace on the bottom, for best. I distinctly remember a very special one, with knitted lace insertion an inch or so wide, with the same matching lace on the bottom. There was always at least one pocket, but usually two large ones.

The white apron was for very special occasions: Relief Society homemaking activities, special quiltings, and parties for the sisters. Sunday afternoon it enhanced Mother's best black dress.

The everyday one, slow to show dirt, was edged all around with bias tape of contrasting color. I was most impressed with

[*]Mae R. Winters was born in Coalville, Utah, of pioneer parents, Edmund and Hannah Chappell Rees, the eleventh of twelve children. She attended Henager School of Business and has held many Church positions; she also served a mission in California. She and her husband, Phares Winters, are parents of four children, 25 grandchildren, and two great-grandchildren. They are members of the Lindon (Utah) Third Ward.

this apron. Its uses were limitless. It made a basket for eggs gathered from the chicken coop, or from a nest found in the tall weeds or grass. Many times Mother would bring in a brood of fluffy yellow chickens in the apron, the bottom edge being brought up to form a temporary nest. The mother hen, squawking and stirring up a fuss, would follow behind. Mother transferred the chickens from a stolen nest to the protection of the stable. The same apron was used, by giving it a swish, to frighten chickens from the flower bed or back porch.

To dry a tear from a child's face, wipe away the dirt, and comfort the children, the apron seemed to be made for this purpose. For a game of hide-and-seek there was never a better place to hide than under the apron, for, with our heads under, and our feet sticking out, we were completely hidden. Kindling and firewood, vegetables and fruit found their way into the kitchen by way of the apron route. When company came unexpectedly, the apron was hastily used as a duster on the dining table or buffet.

Using it for a pot holder to remove hot pans from the stove, the apron was ideal to lift the stove lid off with the aid of the stove lifter, which saved many burned fingers. A flip of the apron would also scatter the flies, as they hovered about the screen at the kitchen door on a fall afternoon. It also served to wipe a perspiring brow after standing at the hot stove all day canning fruit.

Almost everything could be found in the apron pockets: a spool of thread, lost buttons, peppermint candy, cookies, handkerchiefs, bits of paper, a pencil, a piece of string, safety pins, and a coin or two.

For me, there is a never-to-be-forgotten memory of the little ones curled up on Mother's lap as she rocked them and pulled a corner of the big apron over their feet and legs, not alone for warmth, but as a sort of drawing them closer into her wonderful ways.

She was a pioneer mother, with love to go around and around, and her wonderful apron was just one way of showing it.

Tucked away in my chest of memories is one of her ever-useful aprons. In these days of sometimes forgotten aprons, it suggests to me that perhaps my own children and grandchildren have missed some very valuable lessons of life for the lack of a big apron. A very special accessory!

Relief Society Magazine, November 1968, p. 841.

PHOEBE CARTER
WOODRUFF *

"I Dared Not Trust Myself to Say Farewell"

In her characteristic Puritan language she [Phoebe Woodruff] says:

"My friends marveled at my course, as did I, but something within impelled me on. My mother's grief at my leaving home was almost more than I could bear; and had it not been for the spirit within I should have faltered at the last. My mother told me she would rather see me buried than going thus alone out into the heartless world. 'Phoebe,' she said, impressively, 'will you come back to me if you find Mormonism false?' I answered, 'Yes, mother; I will, thrice.' These were my words, and she knew I would keep my promise. My answer relieved her trouble; but it cost us all much sorrow to part. When the time came for my departure I dared not trust myself to say farewell; so I wrote my good-byes to each, and leaving them on my table, ran downstairs and jumped into the carriage. Thus I left the beloved home of my childhood to link my life with the Saints of God.

*Phoebe Carter Woodruff was born in Scarboro, Maine, on March 8, 1807. Her mother was Sarah Fabyan. She joined the Church in 1834, and a year later she joined the Saints in Kirtland, Ohio. She married Wilford Woodruff (who became the fourth president of the Church) in 1836. The mother of several children, she was noted for her faith and loyalty.

"When I arrived in Kirtland I became acquainted with the Prophet Joseph Smith, and received more evidence of his divine mission. There in Kirtland I formed the acquaintance of Elder Wilford Woodruff, to whom I was married in 1836."

Tullidge, *The Women of Mormondom,* pp. 411-13.

SYLVIA PROBST YOUNG[*]

"Gifts From My Mother"

Yesterday, at the home of a friend, I admired a delicately beautiful figu ine. "That," she said proudly, "is a gift from my mother. It v is imported from Italy."

On my way home I thought about the gifts my mother had given me. Materially I don't have much from her—two patchwork quilts she made for me when I was married, an old-fashioned treadle sewing machine, a glass cakestand, a pair of embroidered pillowcases, and a knitting sampler that she made some eighty years ago in a little Swiss school. These things came to me when she died, and moneywise they aren't worth very much. But Mother had left to me some priceless gifts that cannot be bought with money—a legacy for which I am deeply grateful.

My mother taught me to love God's great out-of-doors—the wonder of the seasons, the miracle of a seed, the song of a brook, the return of a bird. Morning after summer morning we worked together in the garden. Her neat rows of vegetables, bordered by

[*]A prolific writer, Sylvia Probst Young has been published extensively in Church magazines as well as the Salt Lake *Tribune* and *Deseret News*. She has taught school in the Jordan School District in Salt Lake County and has also taught in various Church auxiliaries. She and her husband, Reid Young, have four sons, who, like their parents, have all served missions for the Church.

264

sweetpeas and delphinium were admired by friends and neighbors near and far. And how often in the opal twilight we climbed our hill to watch night come softly over the valley.

There was a cold winter morning when we walked across the crusted snow of the meadows to see how the frost had turned the creek and the willows into a regal fairyland.

To mother, books were as essential as bread and butter. She wanted us to know good literature, and we early came to know the works of such writers as Wordsworth and Shakespeare, Longfellow and Lowell.

When a traveling library came to our little town she would see that we borrowed some delightful books for our vacation reading.

The Church magazines—*The Children's Friend, The Juvenile Instructor, The Young Ladies Journal, The Improvement Era,* and *The Relief Society Magazine*—were very carefully kept and at the end of the year we bound these precious volumes with the aid of a paper punch and some shoelaces. There was a special shelf in our clothes closet for these "bound volumes," and we read them over and over again.

Mother had a deep appreciation for good music, and she helped us to gain a love for it. Whenever I think of our front room I remember the corner where the organ stood, and the young people who gathered around it to sing together. Some of us children were always practicing on that old pump organ, and Mother willingly did washings to pay for music lessons.

My mother was deeply spiritual; her family and my father's had come to America for the gospel, and to them it was the most precious thing in the world. We learned about the Lord very early, and we were taught the value and importance of prayer and faith, repentance and baptism, the paying of tithing and the Word of Wisdom.

Our winter nights were spent around a wood-burning stove reading the gospel together. We took turns reading chapters from the Bible and the Book of Mormon. Together, we read the life of Christ from the New Testament, and Joseph Smith's Story. From the Old Testament, we read the stories of all the wonderful old prophets—Moses, Joseph, Samuel, Daniel, or sometimes

Mother told these stories. She loved to tell stories, and she was a wonderful storyteller. Through her teachings we learned the great value of spiritual blessings and gained a knowledge of the truth.

These are some of the gifts my mother gave to me. Time cannot efface them nor can thieves break in and take them from me. These gifts are far more precious than rubies, and for them I shall be eternally grateful to the wonderful woman who was my mother.

Relief Society Magazine, May 1965, pp. 339-40.

ZINA D. YOUNG*

"O Truth, Truth, Truth!"

Zina was about 13 years old. Living as they did within about sixty miles of the Hill Cumorah, they were familiar with the current rumors concerning the bringing forth of the Book of Mormon. Her parents were soon converted to our faith, and the following year Hyrum Smith and David Whitmer visited their home, bringing with them a copy of the first edition of the Book of Mormon. Aunt Zina says: "When I entered the room and read the title of the book that was lying on the window sill, my whole soul was filled with joy. Without opening it I clasped it to my heart and exclaimed, 'O Truth, Truth, Truth!' I knew it had been brought forth by an angel's hand and the feeling that possessed me was one of supreme

*Zina D. H. Young was born January 31, 1821, at Watertown, New York, a daughter of William Huntington and Zina Baker. She was baptized into the Church on August 1, 1835. Shortly after the martyrdom of the Prophet Joseph Smith, she was married to President Brigham Young. In May 1848 she began the journey to the Great Salt Lake Valley. Affectionately known as "Aunt Zina," she was noted for her deep spirituality and pleasing personality. She served as the third general president of the Relief Society; when that organization became affiliated with the National Council of Women in 1891, she became vice-president of the national organization. She was the mother of three children and reared four others. She died August 28, 1901.

ecstasy. From that moment until the present I have never had a doubt of its divinity."

Before these brethren left her home she received the ordinance of baptism at the hands of Hyrum Smith.

Susa Young Gates, *Young Women's Journal*, p. 256.

INDEX

274